Victorian Britain

PETER HEPPLEWHITE
and NEIL TONGE

TEACHER
TIMESAVERS

Published by Scholastic Publications Ltd,
Villiers House,
Clarendon Avenue,
Leamington Spa,
Warwickshire CV32 5PR

© 1995 Scholastic Publications Ltd

Authors Peter Hepplewhite and Neil Tonge
Editor Noel Pritchard
Sub-editors Kate Banham and Joel Lane
Series designer Joy White
Designer Tracey Ramsey
Illustrations Jane Bottomley
Cover illustration Frances Lloyd
Cover photograph Martyn Chillmaid

Advertisement on page 134 reproduced courtesy of Seton Healthcare
Advertisement on page 94 reproduced courtesy of Van Den Bergh Foods
Census reproductions Crown copyright

Designed using Aldus Pagemaker
Printed in Great Britain by Clays Ltd, Bungay, Suffolk

British Library Cataloguing-in-Publication Data
A catalogue record for this book is
available from the British Library.

ISBN 0-590-53303-7

Contents

Introduction

The Victorian period is arguably one of the most attractive (and hence popular) options in primary school History. Many features of this era survive today: it is sufficiently recent for the similarities and differences to be meaningful to children. Artefacts of all kinds are easily found, and there is considerable scope for fulfilling the requirements of the National Curriculum and Scotland's 5-14 Curriculum by studying an extensive range of sources.

The activity sheets in this volume provide a wide range of enjoyable tasks to encourage the development of children's historical thinking and understanding. Many of the activities will be suitable for inclusion in children's work files, to be used for both formative and summative assessments. Most activities are designed to match one of the key elements in the revised orders, and can assist in making 'best fit' level description judgements. The Teachers' Notes suggest extension activities and/or discussion ideas.

About the authors

Neil Tonge is a general adviser and inspector for Newcastle upon Tyne LEA and Peter Hepplewhite is Education Officer for the Tyne and Wear Archive Service.

Rich and poor

As in any period of history, great contrasts existed between the rich and the poor in Victorian society: the titled aristocrat or prosperous business entrepreneur on the one hand, the unwaged and destitute swept into the workhouse on the other. There were gradations, of course: the ranks of the professional middle classes were swelling, and skilled workmen occupied a higher social niche than the unskilled.

The Robertson family If children can trace their own family history, this provides a more meaningful link with the Victorian period; but this can be fraught with difficulties. In place of the real thing an imaginary family tree has been constructed to provide a bridge with the past. It's entirely linear and represents only a single male example from each generation, but will also help to highlight the deficiencies in constructing a version of the past from one point of view. The question 'Who is missing from this family tree?' (the female members of the family, to start with) and the changes in the men's occupations may also provide talking points on the changes in society and the economy.

The Royal family The aim of this activity is to reinforce the link between present and past by tracing the history of the monarchy. Children can place these monarchs in sequence along a timeline (perhaps above and below the timeline given on this sheet) or arrange them as a family tree. This range of options can be used to develop children's understanding of how to arrange information about the past in a variety of meaningful ways. Suggest formats to the children to ensure that they have some clear way of presenting brothers and sisters in a family, such as Edward VIII and George VI. Make sure that the children understand how to read Roman numerals. Children may wish to comment on the style of dress and the manner in which the monarchs are presented, which could lead to some interesting 'Interpretations of the Past' discussions.

A Victorian street scene The picture illustrates a busy street scene in late Victorian England. The purpose of this activity is to develop children's observational skills and to encourage them to consider empathetically the range of thoughts and feelings of different Victorians. This could be developed further as a scenario for drama work, involving the children in writing sketches for characters in the street scene. To make links with another historical period, compare this with a Tudor street scene.

Changing times Children should be able not only to describe differences between 'then' and 'now', but also to appreciate differences within a historical period. This activity is designed with this in mind, but will also encourage pupils to appreciate that the judgement of how things have changed for a particular individual will depend very much on what rung of society the person occupies.

Houses for the rich and the poor The Victorian period was one of social contrasts. Most housing for the poor was built by small speculators who had to produce low-cost housing for a vastly expanding urban population. Under these circumstances, many houses were 'jerry-built' with no piped running water and outside earth closets for toilets, frequently shared by other households. The compulsory purchase of slum property by councils did not come about until after 1870, but little was done to remove public health hazards until the twentieth century. By contrast, the rising middle classes had spacious accommodation which required armies of servants.

Differences in living conditions could clearly lead to differing views on the quality of life at this time, which children could be encouraged to consider. On a more practical level, the illustrations here could be used to design and make models from shoeboxes of the different types of accommodation. Equally, these illustrations can be used as starting-points for creative writing about the families involved.

A rich family and **A poor family** The children can cut out the figures on these sheets, colour them in, and then glue strong card on to the back of each figure. They can then attach a stick to the back of each card, with enough of the stick protruding to serve as a handle. They can make up a short play in which these two families meet one another.

Counting the people: 1 and **2** The first official census in Great Britain did not take place until 1801. Before that date, we can only estimate the population based on a variety of sources including parish registers, bills of mortality and tax returns. Even the first returns of the Civil Census between 1801 and 1831 had their weaknesses. Improvements took place after the Civil

Registration Act of 1837/38, according to which the occupations of all the householders, not merely the head of the family, were required. The absence of a census in 1941 was due to the dislocation of population during World War II.

The first part of this activity is intended to demonstrate the startling rise in population during the reign of Queen Victoria, and to encourage children to consider and research the possible impact of such dramatic increases on housing, transport and jobs.

Comparing Victorian households: 1 and **2** These sheets show the census forms for two households in Glasgow in 1891. They provide opportunities to raise and answer a series of questions about different levels of society. Can the children say which family is the richer? What evidence is there? Describe each household and look at the differences. (Clues: surnames, jobs, servants, rooms.)

In 1841 the census began to collect family details. Since these remain confidential for 100 years, the most recent currently available facts were recorded in 1891. Entries for Victorian streets near your school can be copied from microfilm in your local archives. With this information, it is possible to reconstruct communities in great detail. Entering this on to a database is a useful IT adaptation. The children can then analyse broader patterns such as age profiles or sex ratios. Computer printouts can be a valuable means of organising and communicating source material.

Compiling the census This picture is adapted from an original published in the magazine *Graphic* in 1861. The scenes include a tinker's and a fairground family, a drowned woman, a remote Scottish croft, a slum lodging house and a servant to a wealthy family. The enumerators distributed the census forms, collected them and helped with problems in their completion (much as their modern counterparts do). It would be useful to discuss how errors might have been made. How might someone have been missed? Would anyone have reason to lie?

Filling in the census The blank form gives children an opportunity to conduct their own census. A role play in which an enumerator fills in the form for an illiterate householder makes a lively extension task.

Family accounts and **Family menu** Farm labourers were among the poorest paid workers. Most could not read and write and such accounts are rare. This opens up opportunities for discussion on why it is more difficult to find evidence about the lives of the lower classes of Victorian society. The accounts themselves are annoyingly vague. What was the 'meat'? How much tea did they get for 7d? When the children raise such questions these are ideal openings for making judgements about the usefulness of the source material. If you want to emphasise the £-s-d aspects of the first activity it may be helpful to tackle page 77 first. The Family menu exercise could be reduced to represent one day for less able or younger children.

Escape from the workhouse: 1 and **2** The Poor Law Amendment Act of 1834 linked parishes together to form Poor Law Unions, run by elected boards of Guardians. Each union had to build a workhouse, and most of those asking for poor relief had to enter it. This Act set the pattern for the next 100 years; but from the beginning, it aroused fierce debate. Opponents of the system saw workhouses as degrading; supporters argued that they were a deterrent, inducing able-bodied paupers to look after themselves. It is important to see this legislation in the context of its time: it did provide a system of relief, however grim. Inmates were often better off than many who scraped a living outside, though they were forced to obey the strict rules of the institution.

The 'Escape' story offers an opportunity for creative writing, closely linked to the use of the workhouse plan. The children can use the small details of this to make their narrative more authentic. Reading or writing historical fiction is a lively way of raising children's awareness. The research necessary for a historical novel, film or TV drama could be discussed.

Eating in the workhouse This diet sheet appeared in the First Annual Report of the Poor Law Commissioners (1835), a volume advising on good practice. As such, it was closely followed by unions around the country. It provided cheap, filling meals, but they were grimly monotonous and lacked protein, minerals and vitamins. This exercise offers close links to science and personal and social education.

At work

The Victorian Age saw increasing concern and intervention to improve working conditions. British industry dominated world trade until the 1870s, when rivals such as Germany and the USA began to make their mark.

What is my job? and **Workshop of the world** These occupations and advertisements focus on manufacturing and offer a link to local industries. Adverts can be found in the backs of street directories such as Kelly's (a range of these will be kept by the local studies library or archive). A study of a local company, especially one still surviving today, is an excellent introduction to the cross-curricular theme of Economic and Industrial Understanding.

Water power and **Where should the factory be built?** Britain's main export since the Middle Ages had been woollen cloth but by 1800 cotton had become a serious competitor, and by the end of the nineteenth century it had replaced its rival. Before 1800, most fabrics were made by people working in their homes; then, towards the end of the eighteenth century, machines were invented to spin threads and weave cotton cloth. Powerful water wheels or steam engines powered by coal were needed to make them work. Factories were required to house the machinery. It has to be remembered that the choice of steam engines was not necessarily an obvious one, as water wheels possessed many advantages and, in the early days of steam power, were often more powerful. As a result, the earliest factories were built near to fast-flowing streams, such as those in the Yorkshire and Lancashire Dales. The map could be enlarged and used to develop children's understanding of locational factors in geography.

Dangerous working conditions Factory mills attracted concern because of their size and parents' anxiety for their children. Legislation was enacted in the first half of the nineteenth century to protect children in textile mills, but this largely ignored the vast number of other occupations which employed children. The purpose of the activity is to encourage children to generate their own questions for a historical enquiry. It will also lend itself well to role-play based on interviews between commissioners and factory children.

Factory children There were cases of savage beatings of children, including cases where children were suspended over rotating machinery. In many respects it was a vicious circle. Factory owners were often convinced that the only way they could make a profit was to have machines operating for long hours. Overseers were in fear of losing their jobs if production diminished; chief spinners like Joseph Badder employed the children and thus needed them to meet their requirements; and finally, parents needed the wages so badly that they often overlooked cruelty to their children. This activity lends itself well to role-play. Children should develop from this exercise an awareness that several points of view exist, and appreciate that all the participants are caught in a vicious spiral of economic circumstance.

Children in the coal-mines, My daily routine and **Joseph Taylor's daily routine** Coal-mining was the largest single industry of Victorian Britain. In an age of steam, the country was blessed with ample national resources. Mining was a tough job in hard conditions; but usually, higher than average pay and benefits such as free housing compensated for this.

The words of Joseph Taylor are adapted from the report of the Children's Employment Commission, 1841, which contained interviews with hundreds of children. This caused national outrage and gave Ashley-Cooper, later Lord Shaftesbury, the influence

to persuade Parliament to pass the Mines Act. This barred children younger than 11, and women, from working below ground.

Taylor's words offer opportunities to discuss the usefulness of such evidence. Certainly the mine-owners condemned the interviews as the words of 'ignorant children'. The daily-routine sheets (pages 40 and 41) allow pupils to consider differences between their lives and Joseph's. Intelligent guesses have to be made about some aspects, such as how long he would take to get to work and whether he would have any spare time to play.

Make a model mineshaft: 1 and **2** provides a simple technology activity for younger Key Stage 2 children. This is then extended with a problem-solving exercise. It is likely that the children will suggest something similar to a school register. The method that evolved by the end of the century was the 'tally'. Each man had his own identification number stamped on a brass tag. This was kept on a board with the matching number painted underneath. When a man went underground he took his tally with him and returned it to the board when he came back to the surface. A 'tally boy' kept a check on the system. This was a quick way of telling if anyone had not returned.

A farm labourer's house, The hiring fair, The farming year and **Farm machinery** In 1800, agriculture remained the single most important sector of the economy. Not until 1820 did industrial output exceed that of agriculture, and not until 1850 did agriculture cease to be the biggest employer of labour.

Farm labourers were not only the poorest paid workers, but their cottages were frequently tied (which meant that they came with the job) and the farmer could evict them at will.

All of the activities in this section will develop children's awareness of the problems facing farm workers during Victorian times. Workers were hired and fired as the farmer saw fit. On the sheet 'The hiring fair', the children will have to decide whether they wish to take on all the possible workers. They

could also decide what contracts they would hire them on – for how much and for how long. A group of children could bid against one another to see which workers are more in demand and hence more expensive.

Farm machinery was introduced in response to the need to feed a growing population. It must be remembered that such machinery was expensive and would be more likely to be found on larger farms.

Changing washday This activity offers a basic identification and matching task, looking at the changes in appliances that have transformed domestic chores. It is often possible to borrow Victorian objects from local museum loan collections. Five minutes spent heaving a poss-stick up and down on dirty washing, then wringing out and drying the results, provides a memorable lesson. **NB** A poss-stick or dolly was the wooden implement used to squeeze the dirt out of clothing. It had a handle, a long, thick shaft and a wide base split into three or four sections.

A housemaid's work Domestic service was the largest source of employment for women throughout the nineteenth century. Servants in large houses were graded in status from maid and scullerymaid up to cook and housekeeper. More often, women worked in single-servant households – becoming, at best, almost a friend of the family; or at worst, being sacked when they reached their twenties and replaced by a girl who expected lower wages.

This page is useful as one piece of evidence to stimulate wider research into the position of women. Listing a maid's chores highlights the changes over time in the running of a house. Relying on a real fire for heat and hot water is a fascinating idea for younger children. This can lead to lively interviews with older adults who remember the fire as the centre of family life.

Strike!, Trade unions and **Trade union member** As industrialisation grew, trade unions were established as a means by which workers could protect and improve their interests. They were greatly feared by the ruling classes both as a source of potential revolution and as a restriction upon free trade. Combination Laws were passed in 1799/1800 which made trade unions illegal. Although these laws were repealed in 1825, the unions still endured considerable restrictions on their activities. For this reason, many unions went to great lengths to prove their peaceful pursuit of economic improvement. These activities illustrate the conflict between employer and employee and how trade unions attempted to win legitimacy and respectability. Pupils should develop an awareness of different points of view and possible bias in evidence.

Towns and cities

The growth of the urban population was one of the most startling features of the Victorian period. Towns grew at an alarming rate and without planning. Not only were the administrative facilities of towns and cities inadequate, but most eminent Victorians distrusted and were opposed to government interference. Furthermore, most Victorian builders had very limited resources.

Changes in the locality: 1 and **2** These activity sheets use Ordnance Survey maps (made by the Government map-making organisation) to look at how an area has changed. Although the OS used a variety of scales during the Victorian period, the most useful for primary school work are the 1/2500 (or 25 inches to the mile) sheets. The examples here are redrawn at roughly half this scale, because of limited space, and are not exact. The small numbers on both sheets are spot heights. Local sequential sheets are available from libraries or archives, although the dates of the surveys vary from area to area. This large scale facilitates detailed observations of a locality and can be a valuable support to field work.

Back to back housing: 1 and **2** This activity will enable children to see the pressure on builders to build cheap housing with as few facilities as possible. It must be remembered that the housing of many urban dwellers would have been little better, if not worse, than this. What eventually made the problem most alarming was overcrowding in towns and cities and the spread of infectious diseases. Be sure that the children include alleys between the rows of houses.

Which house do you like? Unless they live in conservation areas, today's house owners are free to change their Victorian houses to suit their own tastes. Some owners value period features and try to retain them, others prefer wholesale modernisation, while many choices are influenced by cost – for example, a new slate roof is very expensive. This exercise asks children not only to pick out how houses have changed, but to give reasons why. Try to follow this up with local fieldwork. Are there any unchanged Victorian houses in a terrace near your school? What changes have been made? What materials have been used? Do estate agents' advertisements give us clues to changes inside houses? Local archives may be able to supply an original building plan and members of local authority conservation teams, usually part of the planning department, are generally willing to talk to schools.

Slum conditions During the Victorian era, cities and towns grew at an unparalleled rate – causing dreadful sanitary conditions, at a time when people were reluctant to intervene. In this example, Dr. Reed was commissioned to enquire into the sanitary conditions of a notoriously poor area of Newcastle called the Sandgate. Only an extract is given here, and you will be able to find other examples relevant to your own area. The purpose of the activity is to illustrate the types of insanitary hazard and to encourage the children to consider how these could be remedied. A discussion on the services now provided would be useful; and an explanation of the Victorians' reluctance to intervene would provide a valuable context to the activity.

Cholera and **Burying the victims: 1** and **2** Cholera is a highly infectious disease which attacks the intestines and causes violent diarrhoea and sickness, cramp, fever and death. The disease micro-organism is spread through impure water. The 'Back to back housing' activity on page 55 is a good preparation for this sheet. The first activity is meant to enable pupils to understand the origins and spread of the disease, and what has since been done to combat it. The statistical activity shows the impact of cholera on a parish in Newcastle and gives pupils some real statistical material to work on. (To understand the nature of the cholera epidemic, however, the children would need appropriate historical and medical descriptions – the death statistics alone are not enough.) The question marks by some of the entries mean that the compiler was unsure of the information. For ease, when calculating weekly totals, start the week on a Friday.

Make a Victorian shopping street: 1 and **2** This activity can lead to a colourful classroom frieze or stand-up model. Many Victorian streets were built by speculative builders over a number of years and are not uniform in appearance. The children can decide which type of shop they want, how to decorate the windows and the design of a suitable sign. Comparing window dressing then and now can lead to a design-focused discussion.

Trouble with toilets Ash closets replaced cess pits and midden heaps in Victorian towns from the middle of the century onwards. In working-class districts, in particular, they remained the main form of sanitation well into the 1920s and '30s. WCs were available, but many councils were reluctant to take on the expense of laying adequate water supplies or sewers. The inconvenience of using outside toilets during the night made the chamber pot a household object. Asking the children to describe what it would have been like to use an ash closet on a cold, snowy winter's evening can be an interesting starting-point.

Spotting Victorian street names Names can be a useful clue in dating Victorian streets and an interesting starting-point for personal research. Investigating a name provides a real-life puzzle of manageable proportions. Group or individual work could be presented as part of a 'Why is this street called...?' display. Street names are an interpretation of the past. What kind of people or events are remembered? What kind are ignored? Why are there no streets with 'cholera' associations?

Street furniture Most Victorian street furniture has now disappeared, but it is worth noting any surviving local examples and incorporating them into fieldwork. Compare the items on the worksheets with modern street furniture near your school. Asking the children to describe how the objects were used encourages them to make deductions from historical sources.

Who lived or worked here? Street directories are ideal for historical enquiry. They are available for most years of the Victorian period for most areas. For the last question, it would be helpful if you chose a local street in advance and had photocopies of records available. A comparison could be made with other local sources such as the census (see page 24). Which document is the most useful for investigating the history of a street? What are the advantages and disadvantages of each type of document?

At school

It was a slow process for English Victorians to recognise the importance of education for the humbler classes. (The Scots took the issue more seriously, and most villages had schools paid for from the rates.) Many early elementary schools were run by religious organisations, dominated by their various tenets of faith. The National Society was founded in 1811 by Church of England followers, and the British and Foreign Schools Society by Nonconformists in 1808. State involvement began with minor grants to support this voluntary system. By the late 1850s this had reached such a level that committees were appointed to assess value for money.

Many of the tasks in this chapter can be combined to plan a 'Victorian Schoolroom' session in which children could dress up in role, perform the activities and experience a harsher school environment.

Then and now The aim here is to encourage fieldwork in the children's own environment. They can quickly become experts on their own school, evaluating it in comparison with the design on the activity sheet. Ideally, this will move beyond the obvious, such as outside v. inside toilets or different materials, to considering the aesthetics of each building. Do they prefer the new or old design, flat or pitched roofs, big or small windows? Can they explain their preferences?

Going to the Ragged School: 1 and **2** This looks in detail at one example of a major philanthropic movement, once again involving Lord Shaftesbury. As well as reducing crime, what other reasons might there be for educating young children? Tragically for the Newcastle teacher, the school opened just as a major cholera epidemic hit the city. Here is your chance to impress your children with the dedication of teachers. Their own suggestions for dealing with recalcitrant pupils may be enlightening.

Punish the child Classroom regimes were often harsh. It is important that children understand some of the reasons for this – class sizes, expectations and attitudes towards children – and also realise that not all schoolmasters were cruel, as in the example of the teacher from the Ragged School in Newcastle.

Problem child This story starting-point provides opportunities for creative writing as well as a scenario for a re-enactment of a Victorian classroom. Pupils could be divided into those who wish to see the problem child go into school to face the wrath of the schoolmaster, those who decide he will wander the town or those who want the child to go to his parents.

Dressing for school These pictures will provide a starting-point for comparing Victorian children's clothes with those worn today. Boys can tuck their trousers into their socks and wear a flat cap to look the part; a long skirt, blouse and shawl will transform the girls.

Educating girls The education of middle-class girls was in preparation for marriage, not a career. In the humbler classes, for both males and females,

learning was at worst a dangerous experience; at best it was a moral crusade against crime, or it provided a trade confirming their station in life.

The Inspector's visit This focuses on the day that teachers dreaded each year, the HMI inspection on which grants depended. The children would have been put through their paces and were under considerable pressure to perform well. The grant system was blamed for much of the uninspiring rote learning that went on in classrooms. This activity emphasises different points of view and the importance of captions to explain the context of an illustration.

Prepare a lesson This sheet offers a research task which may be presented to others when completed. The children will need to consider how to communicate their findings, as well as the content. They could be encouraged to use modern technology such as OHP transparencies or computer-generated 'flashcards' for new words.

Pounds, shillings and pence A fun activity which shows how pre-decimal coins can be used as sources of evidence in their own right and for maths games. Pennies and halfpennies can still be bought cheaply from coin dealers. The coins illustrated here provide a small sample of the main coins in circulation, including those of higher value. Children can do a wide range of computation exercises with this money, which can also be used in the play corner set up as a Victorian sweet shop or schoolroom.

Recitation: 1 and **2** Children should concentrate on learning C. J. Coleridge's poem by heart and reciting it with fluency and emotion. It would also be useful to look at this as a piece of evidence for the personality cult that was built around the figure of the Queen. This was the popular image that many Victorians adored. The past is interpreted to support the present.

Handwriting practice This is a fun exercise which has a miraculous effect on noisy classes. If you are feeling brave enough, provide quill pens, ink and blotting paper. Felt-tipped calligraphy pens are an acceptable alternative. Remember, if each letter is not in the right place on the right line, the sentence must be repeated. This activity can be one element of a Victorian schoolday re-enactment.

Transport

Changes in transport 1840-1900 Industrialisation brought with it rapid changes in the transportation of goods. At the beginning of the nineteenth century our road network was still based on the inheritance left from the Roman conquest – roads were ribbons of rutted mud in winter and dust bowls in summer. Some improvement had taken place due to the establishment of turnpike trusts – private companies that could charge tolls on stretches of road leased to the trust – and the carrying of bulky goods on canals. The greatest transport phenomenon, however, came with the building of the Stockton to Darlington railway in 1825, and by 1850 the present railway network was established. Railways were fast, reliable and efficient, representing the hallmark of the modern age. It must be remembered that railways did not mean the end of the horse and carriage, for even greater numbers of these were needed to transport goods and people to or from railway stations.

Which form of travel? These pictures illustrate different forms of travel available in the nineteenth century, although it must be remembered that railways made most forms of long-distance transport redundant. Canals were victims along with coaching companies, although both lingered on (at least into the 20th century) by carrying bulky goods where time was not of the essence. This activity encourages children to assess and evaluate the respective merits of each form of transport, and to deduce the ultimate advantages of railway travel.

Travel by road and **Getting faster** Horse-drawn transport had been the norm for thousands of years. However, with the increasing need for passengers and goods to be transported quickly in an industrialised country, during Victorian times transport improved considerably. None the less, travel could

still be hazardous and views on the relative merits and disadvantages of the new forms of transport varied. These activities encourage children to consider a variety of viewpoints and experiences, some of which could be used in a travel diary.

Canals: advantages and **Canals: disadvantages** The carriage of bulky goods was a time-consuming and expensive process. Although canals had been constructed in Roman times, it was not until the eighteenth century that the gathering momentum of the Industrial Revolution gave canal building a new impetus. The first canal to be built in this new wave of construction was the Bridgewater Canal, designed and built by Joseph Brindley. There followed a 'mania' for canal building which reached a peak in the 1790s, but by 1815 the network was largely finished. Canals still continued to carry goods throughout the nineteenth century, but only where the carriage of goods did not require swift delivery.

These two activities enable children to examine the evidence to find reasons for the emergence and decline of canals as a transport system, and trace change and progress over time.

Railways: for and against The advent of rail travel was not greeted with enthusiasm by everyone. For a variety of reasons, as illustrated in the extracts, people both feared and were hostile towards the railways. In some instances this opposition was a pretext to squeeze more cash compensation from railways, particularly by landowners across whose land the railway companies desired to build.

This activity encourages children to consider a variety of viewpoints and to understand that notions of progress are frequently subjective. It can be used as a stimulus to empathetic understanding.

Race against time Stage coaches originally tried to compete with the railways. Early trains could travel at about 25-30 miles per hour, but they often had to take slightly longer routes to avoid very steep hills or to cross rivers. A stage coach, in good weather, could travel at about 20 miles per hour if it could get

fresh horses at the posting stations. This activity commemorates the coaching companies' doomed attempts to fight against progress.

Building a railway This enjoyable activity is designed for Key Stage 1 children, with three purposes in mind. Firstly, to develop vocabulary associated with railway construction – children will need help with this, and a word wall of the terms with an illustration from the activity would be useful. Secondly, children will be encouraged to consider the various construction features that are necessary to build a railway. Finally, they must solve the problem of building the railway by choosing the correct construction feature.

Railway routes: 1 and **2** After the opening of the Liverpool to Manchester Railway in 1830, a 'railway mania' began with proposed lines radiating out all over Britain. The railways were not state-owned: private companies battled with one another to win routes, and some joined together in an attempt to dominate the system.

This activity should be played in pairs. It simulates the cost of building lines and the need to choose suitable routes in the anticipation of profit; this involves planning, problem solving and number work.

The Empire

The British Empire, 1897 The Empire had grown gradually during the nineteenth century. However, from the 1870s onwards, imperial conquests came thick and fast. The expanding Empire seemed to demonstrate British greatness; but ironically, as Britain began to celebrate its world influence, the real source of its power, industrial production, was already being lost to Germany and the USA.

This activity encourages children to be aware of the scope of the Empire and Britain's involvement in world affairs. There could be a useful link here with the study of a developing country in geography, for example India or Egypt.

A trading empire This activity looks at a long-term incentive for British imperialism – profit. In this advertisement, the white tea planter stands in the foreground, confidently in charge of his workforce. This is a perfect piece of propaganda for the Empire – an ordered and prosperous scene managed by the British. An extension task could be to look at this scene from the viewpoint of a native worker and to explore how the indigenous economy suffered at the expense of the highly profitable plantations.

A victory for the Empire In 1898, Britain began a war in South Africa against the Boers. These people were descendants of Dutch settlers and wanted to set up their own country rather than be ruled by the British. It took over 250,000 soldiers from all over the Empire to defeat the much smaller Boer army. When the Boer capital, Pretoria, was finally captured, there were huge celebrations all over Britain.

This activity shows imperial hysteria at its height. People felt that all was still well with the Empire, but in fact the Boer War had been a catalogue of disasters. The log book extract shows the important role that schools had in fostering 'patriotism'.

Leaving the Highlands: 1 and **2** This activity focuses on an emotive episode in Scottish history. During the 1840s, thousands of highlanders were driven off their land by landlords who wanted to turn their farms into grazing land for sheep, which was more profitable. This caused such national outrage that many landlords had to switch from policies of eviction to quiet encouragement to move.

The activity encourages children to empathise with the highlanders. Pupils could be asked why people might not always say what they are thinking. For example, the highlander may be trying to encourage his distraught wife while hiding his own grief. The children should share their individual work in groups and move on to perform a short drama in which the couple confront their landlord.

Pity the poor emigrant This sheet looks at the grim circumstances of the potato famine in Ireland. In 1847, 110,000 Irish people were forced to emigrate to Canada alone and 140,000 to the USA. The quarantine facilities on arrival were swamped – tens of thousands were allowed through with only a brief glance as doctors walked by the passengers lined up on deck. Even so, by June 1847, 1,800 sick emigrants had been crowded into quarantine hospitals, sheds and tents. Many of those who passed quarantine were still ill and spread typhoid to settlements across Canada. The only hope of survival for Sean and his mother, the characters on the activity sheet, would have been to find work in Quebec or Montreal.

An arrogant empire This activity highlights the deep racism that grew with the British Empire. There were a number of reasons for this – attitudes formed by the slave trade; technological and military superiority; fundamentalist Christianity which portrayed other faiths as heathen; the feeling of betrayal and outrage at the Indian mutiny in 1857. However, the British had not always been like this. During the early years of the East India Company, brown and white people had mixed socially and intermarried. This worksheet offers an opening for discussion on interpretations of the past. Why did *Robinsoe Crusoe* suit Victorian tastes?

Words from the Empire This activity encourages children to examine one legacy of the Empire. It shows that the English language is not fixed but is lively and changing. It can also be used to show Britain as a multicultural nation. The India of the Victorian Empire has now become Bangladesh, Pakistan and India. Provide suitable dictionaries for the children to use, such as the *Collins School Dictionary*.

Queen Victoria's Diamond Jubilee Parade (1897): 1 and **2** This event was a deliberate statement of British greatness. Fifty thousand troops took part in the parade on 22 June 1897. The *Daily Mail* commented, 'How many millions of years has the sun stood in heaven? But the sun never looked down until yesterday upon the embodiment of so much energy and power.' To take this beyond a simple colouring-in exercise, it would be useful to ask why troops from so many colonies were included and why native troops such as the Dyaks were so popular with the crowds.

Inventions and discoveries

Many of our modern inventions and conveniences originated in the Victorian period, which (like our own) was 'gadget mad'. This inventiveness was a direct consequence of industrialisation and the emphasis placed on technological progress.

Much of this section will focus on technological activities related to Victorian inventions, so it would be helpful to provide construction kits and materials.

Before and after The purpose of this activity is to highlight the important inventions and to encourage children to place them in a historical context. This range of technological developments could be extended, particularly in the field of medicine (see pages 111 and 112).

Messages in Morse Code The most famous Morse signal is SOS, the international call of distress: as preparation for this activity, the children could try tapping it on their desk top – 3 quick taps, 3 slow taps, 3 quick taps. Morse Code was developed for the telegraph, but continued in use long after radio became popular. The Victorians created the first electronic 'information highway'. A telegraph cable was laid under the English Channel in 1850 and under the Atlantic in 1866.

Electrical experiments The harnessing of electrical power was the phenomenon of the age and was destined to transform the twentieth century. In 1831, Michael Faraday conducted experiments in which the properties of electro-magnetism came to be applied to powering machinery. Experiments with electric lighting began in the latter half of the nineteenth century. Almost simultaneously, Thomas Edison and Joseph Swan developed the incandescent filament light bulb – a heated filament that would illuminate inside a glass bulb filled with an inert gas. The experiment can be extended with the addition of switches and circuit breakers. In historical terms, children can list all the uses of electrical power today and what preceded its application. Electrical circuits are part of the Science National Curriculum requirements at Key Stage 2.

Lighting a house This sheet looks at the main developments in domestic lighting, though it should be remembered that many people, especially in rural areas, had nothing but candles and oil lamps until well into this century. The slaughter of whales for high-quality lamp oil may make an interesting discussion point. Burning a gas camping light with and without the mantle effectively demonstrates the way in which this small piece of gauze dramatically improves the light level.

Make a pinhole camera Photography made its appearance in the late 1830s and opened a whole new way of perceiving and capturing the world. Drawing or writing were the only ways to represent scenes or people before this. Equipment and techniques were cumbersome, and it is a remarkable achievement that some of the most exquisite early photographs were produced in remote parts of the world and under difficult circumstances.

This activity relates well to either science or technology, and the inversion of the image gives rise to considerable debate. Victorian photographs can still be found and much can be learned from them. The value and limitations of photographic evidence, in contrast with other types of evidence, can profitably be discussed. Pictures of Victorian photographers using their cameras can be a useful introduction.

Make a string telephone The invention of the telephone by Alexander Graham Bell in 1876 was preceded by the electric telegraph; but with the adaptation of a vibrating diaphragm within the mouthpiece of a hand set, the human voice could be heard over considerable distances. This activity represents a familiar topic on 'sound' in science. In historical terms, children could be asked to comment on the impact of such an invention and which groups of people it would be most likely to affect.

Moving pictures: 1 and **2** Early cinema fell just outside this historical period, but the Victorians were

well on their way towards providing the foundations of the invention.

This activity could be well grounded in a topic on 'light' in science and fulfils many of the requirements of technology. Teacher guidance is required.

Milestones in medicine: 1 and **2** This sheet presents a series of medical breakthroughs to be re-arranged in chronological order. Encourage the children to look for links between developments over time and to consider the way in which scientific discoveries build on one another. Comparing Victorian breakthroughs in medicine with those of Ancient Greece is a useful way of making links across periods.

The *Great Britain* Here we look at the achievements of Isambard Kingdom Brunel. This ship was built for service between England and Australia. The first voyage took 83 days and she carried 142 crew and 630 passengers. The worksheet emphasises technical innovation – adapting existing ideas on a grander scale. Drawing the full-size propeller can be an excellent group task for a fine day, with the children drawing a rough and ready circle using a length of string attached to a central point.

Sail or steam? While Trevithick, Hedley and Stephenson were using steam power to drive locomotives, other engineers, most notably Brunel, were experimenting with steam-powered iron ships. The first successful steamship was the *Comet* in 1815. Improvements were made, but the biggest sailing ships (called 'clippers') were still faster than steam ships in the second half of the nineteenth century. In 1865-66, the *Great Eastern* helped to lay telegraph cables across the Atlantic; but on the far eastern runs sailing ships were still faster. However, with the opening of the Suez Canal the supremacy of steam was proven. Children can experiment with a variety of powered ships in order to determine which they regard as the most efficient. In a historical setting, children could argue the respective merits of steam and sail and list the advantages that the development of steam power would bring.

All mod cons! Much of the technology familiar today sprang from the Victorian period. Alexander Graham Bell demonstrated the telephone in 1876, and by the end of the century many businesses and wealthy individuals were linked by a nationwide telephone network. The first typewriter was devised by C.L. Sholes in 1867 and produced commercially by Remington in 1874. The QWERTY keyboard is still used as the standard computer keyboard. The 'safety' bicycle was developed in 1885 and the pneumatic tyre in 1888. Edison and Swan buried their differences over who invented the light bulb to launch the Edison and Swan United Electric Light Co. in 1884.

Religion

During the Victorian period in Britain, the Christian religion was the dominant source of beliefs about life. As such, it was regarded as a means by which social values could be taught.

All things bright and beautiful Many Victorian hymns display the social values of their time, and classwork could be extended by an examination of other hymns. Although it is a difficult exercise, children could be encouraged to give a closer reading to Victorian literature for the underlying social messages it contains.

Religious ABC and **Religious numbers** A perfect example of an integrated syllabus. All aspects of the curriculum were used to illustrate Christian knowledge and precepts.

Victorian Christmas: 1 and **2** and **Christmas cards** The Victorians enjoyed the sentimentality of Christmas, and many of our accepted traditions began in the Victorian period. Children could be encouraged to bring in collections of modern-day Christmas cards with Victorian themes to be used for an Interpretations of the Past exercise. Teacher guidance will be needed to make the tree. The template for the tree can be enlarged on the photocopier in order to make a larger tree.

Christian duty This sheet emphasises one of the most positive features of Victorian religion. In an age before the welfare state, charities helped millions of people. In many cases, the running and funding of these charities gave upper- and middle-class women an important role in public life. This enabled them to build influence and develop the range of skills which they used in their campaign for the right to vote (eventually achieved in 1918). This activity paves the way for an investigation of local sources. Street directories often list charities under 'Benevolent Institutions'. Many charities also produced annual reports listing those making donations and activities for the year.

The demon drink The Temperance Movement was one of the most powerful moral crusades of the Victorian era. The abuse of alcohol was widespread, especially amongst the urban working classes, and was blamed for many social problems. The campaign was widespread and compelling, with temperance magazines, meetings, missions, travelling lantern shows and temperance halls and hotels. The Temperance Movement illustrates how religious beliefs could be carried through to personal conduct. However, abstainers were the victims of ridicule and were often portrayed as hypocrites in literature. This activity emphasises one interpretation of drinking and its effects. To extend this, the children could be asked how a pub owner or a brewer might have felt about the Temperance Movement. Equally, what would a temperance TV advertisement look like?

Graveyard studies, **Graveyard inscriptions** and **Memorial stones** offer opportunities for local fieldwork. Churchyards and cemeteries allow the children to investigate, collect, organise and present their own information. Problems such as trying to read partially erased headstones add an air of mystery. Most children find themselves emotionally involved with the tasks at some point, perhaps on seeing a family grave which lists the deaths of young children. Display materials can be prepared quickly by taking wax rubbings of inscriptions. Information can be analysed in an IT data-handling exercise

under field headings such as forename, surname, age, occupation, date of death, date of birth and cause of death. Be careful to check that visits are allowed, and what the restrictions are.

Leisure

Despite the conventional picture of long working hours, the pursuit of leisure activities increased during the Victorian age. From high culture to low entertainment, all had their place and social significance.

A Victorian holiday This activity asks children to make deductions and support their answers with reference to the evidence. They are also invited to pose further questions for whose answers the evidence is limited.

A seaside holiday This involves careful observation, identification and annotation of features. There is scope to extend this activity by comparing the traditional seaside holiday with modern attractions. Local seaside towns could be discussed or visited. Although considerable freedom was allowed to children, men and women changed in the privacy of wheeled huts and had their own sectors of beach. A tanned complexion was not fashionable and ladies used umbrellas to protect themselves from the sun.

Wish you were here This could be used for a short piece of writing, drawing upon knowledge acquired from the previous two worksheets. Children will need to plan their writing carefully due to restrictions of space. One of the cheapest souvenirs of a trip to the seaside was a postcard. These could be posted with a ½d stamp, half the price of sending a letter. It is well worth collecting a few Victorian postcards for discussion or as part of a school museum. Postcards became so popular that it was common for photographers to present prints in a postcard format, ready to be sent to friends and relatives.

Victorian parks Parks were often given to a community by a wealthy landowner or businessman or bought by the local council. They were seen as the 'lungs' of cities. They offered relaxation in pleasant

surroundings for workers in the crowded and smoky towns. This task is appropriate for local history studies and can be used to support fieldwork.

For sale This activity should provide an opportunity for children to look in detail at the interiors of Victorian houses and dolls' houses, both on visits to museums and through reference books. Once the activity is completed, the contrasts of 'upstairs' and 'downstairs' can be discussed and re-enacted.

Making Victorian figures Apart from developing children's manipulative skills, the figures themselves will provide opportunities for creative play – one scenario has been suggested. The purpose of the task is to encourage children to contrast the lives and expectations of the rich and poor in Victorian Britain.

What sport are they playing? This identifies six games that gained mass popularity during the Victorian period. Indeed, it is sometimes said that Britain's greatest cultural exports were sports such as cricket, rugby and football. By the 1870s, for example, Association Football had become a spectator sport among the urban working classes. By the 1880s, all the modern features of the game were present, such as permanent grounds, leagues of teams, admission charges and even hooliganism. This task asks children to recognise the sporting activities in spite of the different clothing. To extend this, children might cut up the sheet and match the Victorian players to modern equivalents cut from a newspaper or magazine.

Women and sport Victorian women were expected to be good housewives and mothers. They had to fight to gain the same rights as men. One way of doing this was to show that they were not weak and helpless – as men liked to think. By the end of Queen Victoria's reign many women were taking part in sports. These Elliman's advertisements are clearly focusing on an image of the 'modern' woman, determined and vigorous. Women's mobility, however, remained relatively restricted by their clothing. What do the poses and facial expressions of the women in the advertisements tell us? An extension task might involve looking at the images of women in advertisements today, especially those concerned with sporting products.

A street game This sheet looks back to a time when children played in the street and invented their own games for amusement. As this example shows, the rules could be complicated and taking part demanded reasonable fitness. Does this game, or something similar, survive in the playground today? Some schools have deliberately revived the playing of traditional schoolyard games. It might be interesting to record those games played currently and compare them with the games played by parents and grandparents. Can the children suggest how and why such games have changed?

Arts and culture

The nineteenth century saw a great variety of artistic styles. Two styles predominated, and were fiercely defended by their respective supporters. Some artists favoured a continuation of the classical style, with mathematically conceived balances and proportions. Others took their inspiration from the Middle Ages, seeing in its tall Gothic spires a symbol of the aspirations of humanity.

Victorian paintings Grand historical subjects were usually the themes of early paintings, whereas in the latter half of the century a whole host of art styles flourished – particularly Impressionism. These artists could well be linked to the Art National Curriculum requirement to study past artists and their styles. Of more popular interest were the Victorian moralist painters, whose work is invaluable not only for details of dress and buildings but for attitudes and perceptions.

This illustration is based on a painting entitled 'Applicants for Admission to a Casual Ward' (1874) by Sir Luke Fildes. Note the well-dressed woman in the foreground of the picture and the interest taken in her by the elderly gentleman and policeman. No doubt she is going to be rescued into the security of the middle classes.

Victorian writers The Victorian age produced some wonderful writers, who wrote vividly of their age and for all times. Such works provide us, at one level, with descriptions of clothes, houses and customs of the time, and at a deeper level, with a picture of Victorian attitudes and values. Many novelists also regarded part of their craft as being to illuminate the foibles and evils of their own age, in order that they should be reformed. The 'Condition of England' novels were very popular as vehicles for social reform, pointing out as they did the disparities between rich and poor. Whether they were always read in this vein is, of course, doubtful as they were hugely enjoyable stories in their own right, providing a safe glimpse of the 'other side of life' for middle-class readers.

Victorian books: 1 and **2** These activities, it is hoped, will encourage children to read these novelists further for their literary merit as well as for their social documentation of the Victorian Age. Providing a dictionary will help with any difficult words. Children can be asked how true these works of fiction are, and this provides an excellent starting-point for investigation. The children could read *Oliver Twist* and then answer questions such as 'Why were there workhouses? Were they all like this?' in order to give motivation, purpose and direction to the study of the period.

The battle of the styles This activity looks at the Victorian passion for ornamented buildings. Architects often copied from other countries and periods, arguing over what was 'proper' for important buildings. On one side were those who preferred the classical style that had developed steadily all over Europe since the Renaissance, reaching its peak in the eighteenth century. On the other were those who, in the spirit of the Romantic movement in art, literature and music, declared that medieval Gothic was the most inspiring style. The children are asked to investigate the two styles and the terms associated with them. The worksheet can be a starting-point for studying local buildings and the legacy of Ancient Greece.

Back in fashion The 'Victoriana' style is extremely popular, and carries with it impressions of a lost, more certain age when craft skills had not yet degenerated into DIY. In fact, the Victorians were ardent collectors of mass-produced articles which they believed reflected former glories – both classical and Gothic.

This activity is intended to introduce children to the difficult concept of 'Interpretations of the Past' – how one age selectively interprets another. They should have great fun hunting through catalogues to discover further examples of Victoriana – but make sure they are not sidetracked into choosing birthday and Christmas presents. Through this exercise, they will begin to understand how one age 'borrows' from another. The more astute may begin to see why some things are borrowed while others are rejected, and to consider what this selectivity tells us about our own age and values.

Victorian street slang This activity looks at a few common phrases from the late nineteenth century. Most are no longer in use, illustrating how language changes from period to period, especially non-standard English. These examples can be put together to make an amusing piece of extended writing. Reading an extract from a Sherlock Holmes story can provide an interesting starting-point for the crime story.

Make a music hall: 1 and **2** The music hall was the chief form of mass entertainment in mid- to late-Victorian Britain. This activity is intended to give children creative opportunities to devise programmes of entertainment to perform for other children in the class. Copies of popular Victorian songs are easily obtainable and, of course, provide a source in their own right, as well as helping to fulfil the general requirements of the National Curriculum for History by providing a variety of source materials. Teacher guidance will be needed for the practicalities of constructing the music hall and the music hall characters.

Name _____

The Robertson family

These pictures show some of the members of the Robertson family. Underneath each picture you will see two dates. The first date tells you the year in which they were born and the second tells you the year in which they died.

✤ Cut out each of the pictures and the timeline at the bottom of this page.

✤ Arrange the pictures in order on the timeline according to the year in which each person was born.

✤ Why do you think the sort of jobs done by the Robertsons has changed?

✤ Which people are missing from this family tree?

Wayne Robertson
1982 - still living
At school.

Andrew Robertson
1932 - still living
Became a worker in an electronics factory in the South of England.

James Robertson
1878 - 1946
Jacob's son. Moved to the North-East of England to work as a coal miner.

Jacob Robertson
1850 - 1925
A farm worker who left Ireland to live in Scotland in 1872.

Neil Robertson
1906 - 1991
Became a car worker in Coventry.

1830	1840	1850	1860	1870	1880	1890	1900	1910	1920	1930	1940	1950	1960	1970	1980	1990

A timeline

The Royal family

❖ Cut out the pictures of the kings and queens and the timeline at the bottom of this page.

❖ Arrange the pictures in order on the timeline according to the years that they reigned.

❖ How many monarchs have there been since Queen Victoria? How long did each of them reign?

❖ Is Queen Elizabeth II the granddaughter, great-granddaughter or great-great-granddaughter of Queen Victoria?

George V
(1910 - 1936)

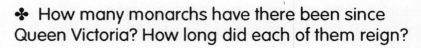

Queen Victoria
(1837 - 1901)

Edward VIII
(1936)

George VI
(1936 - 1952)

Elizabeth II
(1952 to present)

Edward VII
(1901 - 1910)

1830	1840	1850	1860	1870	1880	1890	1900	1910	1920	1930	1940	1950	1960	1970	1980	1990

Name _____

A Victorian street scene

Victorian streets were lively places. Carriages, street sellers, rich businessmen on their way to appointments and poor people begging could all be seen.

✣ Look carefully at the street scene below.

✣ Who are the rich and who are the poor people in the picture? Explain why you think this. Look carefully at their clothes and what they are doing.

✣ What might they be thinking about each other?

Street scenes

Changing times

Queen Victoria ruled Britain for 64 years and during this long period there were many changes.

✤ Look at the two street scenes below. The first picture shows what it was like in the early years of

Victoria's reign. The second picture shows the same street just before she died.

✤ What differences can you see between the pictures?

Houses for the rich and the poor

Poor people lived in small houses. Some of these houses had narrow alleys between them at the back. A rich family's house was much larger and more comfortable.

♣ Make a list of all the differences you can see between the two houses.

Clothing

A rich family

A poor family

The census

Counting the people: 1

The total number of people living in a country is called its population. The counting of the population is known as taking a census. On a particular day, details of the people in every house in the country are recorded, including their ages, jobs and where they were born. The very first census was taken in 1801 and has taken place every ten years since then except for 1941.

✤ Look at the information below and complete the graph on Counting the people: 2. Colour in each figure to represent one million people. The first one has been done for you.

Year	Population
1841	18 million
1851	21 million
1861	23 million
1871	25 million
1881	30 million
1891	33 million
1901	37 million

✤ How many more people were there in 1901 than in 1841?

✤ During which decade does the biggest increase in population take place?

✤ How do you think the lives of people would have changed because of the increase in population?

Counting the people: 2

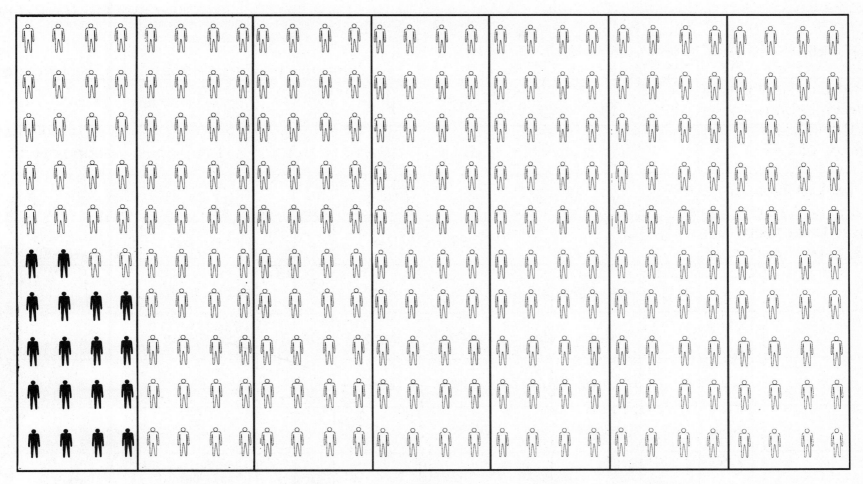

| 1841 | 1851 | 1861 | 1871 | 1881 | 1891 | 1901 |

The census

Comparing Victorian households: 1									

Road, street Number or name of house	Houses		Name and surname of each person	Relation to head of family	Condition as to marriage	Age last birthday		Rank, profession or occupation	Where born	Rooms with one or more windows
	Inhab-ited	Unin-habited				M	F			
153, Glasgow St.	1		Mary Murray	Head	Unm.		60	Lodging house keeper	Ireland	4
			Margaret Armstrong	Adopted dau.	Unm.		20	Domestic servant	Lanarkshire	
			Francis Murray	Nephew	Unm.	34		Quay labourer	Ireland	
			Thomas Elliot	Boarder	Unm.	44		Pensioner	Lanarkshire Glasgow	
			John McKenzie	Boarder	Unm.	26		Wood turner	Edinburghshire Tranent	
			Michael Walsh	Boarder	Unm.	48		Cork cutter	Ireland	
			Michael Walsh	Boarder	Unm.	21		Slater	Ireland	
			Edward Little	Boarder	Unm.	44		Cabinet maker	Ireland	
			John M. Langholm	Boarder	Unm.	39		Soap boiler	Ireland	
			John Carmichael	Boarder	Unm.	30		Quay labourer	Ireland	

Comparing Victorian households: 2

Road, street Number or name of house	Houses		Name and surname of each person	Relation to head of family	Condition as to marriage	Age last birthday		Rank, profession or occupation	Where born	Rooms with one or more windows
	Inhab-ited	Unin-habited				M	F			
Glasgow Terrace	1		William Pearce	Head	Mar.	48		Engineer and shipbuilder. Employs 5000 men and boys	England	17
			Dinah E. Pearce	Wife	Mar.		44		England	
			Edward H. Beckles	Visitor	Mar.	65		Bishop Church of England	Barbados	
			John Miller	Servant	Unm.	22		Butler	Lanarkshire	
			Mary Bell	servant	Wid.		62	Housekeeper	Ireland Co. Tyrone	
			Janet Dalrimple	servant	Unm.		42	Cook	Wigtonshire Glenluce	
			Mary M. McAlister	servant	Unm.		28	Lady's maid	Ayrshire Irvine	
			Allison S. Smith	servant	Unm.		17	Housemaid	Midlothian Musselborough	
			Isabella McDonald	servant	Unm.		22	kitchenmaid	Argyleshire Mull	

The census

Compiling the census

These pictures show some of the adventures of enumerators (the people who collected the census information) in 1861.

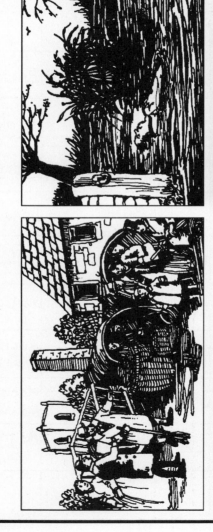

♣ Choose one picture and write a short newspaper article to go with it. Think about how the enumerator travelled, what he saw, said, smelled and thought about the people he visited.

♣ Draw your own picture of the enumerator speaking to the captain of a ship and collecting the details of the crew.

Name _____

Filling in the census

♣ Imagine you are the head of the household. Invent your own Victorian family and fill in the information on the form.

Number of house	Road/street & number or name of house	Inhab-ited	Unin-hab-ited	Name and surname of each person	Relation to head of family	Condition as to marriage	Age last birthday		Rank, profession or occupation	Where born
							M	F		

Spending money

Family accounts

John Allen worked on a farm as a labourer in Northumberland in 1841. There were seven people in his family and their income was 19s 5d (97p) a week.

✤ Add up the Allens' shopping bill. Work out the total for each week first and then add these together. Can you work this out in new and old money? Remember 12d = 1s and 20s = £1.

✤ Look at the total spent and compare this with the Allens' weekly income. What problems do you think they would have had? What could they have done about it?

✤ Use the Family menu worksheet to plan the meals for a week for the Allens and compare this with the meals your own family eats in a week. (Helpful hint: John had a large garden and would be able to grow his own vegetables.)

✤ What are the main differences between your diet and the Allens'?

date	articles bought	old money £	s	d	new money p
26 April – 2 May	4st flour		10	7	52½
	oatmeal		1	1½	6
	sugar			8	3
	soap			6	2½
	coffee			6	2½
	meat		5	11	28½
	butter			6	2½
	milk		2	0	10
	tea			10	4
	cotton		1	0	5
	eggs			2½	1
	yeast			2½	1
	total				
3 May – 10 May	4st flour		10	7	52½
	1lb soap			6	2½
	meat		3	0	15
	leather (for coat)		2	7	12½
	2lb sugar		1	2½	6
	tea			7	2½
	paper			6	2½
	comb			6	2½
	yeast			2¼	1
	milk			4	1½
	eggs			2½	½
	potatoes		3	7	17½
	coal		6	6	32½
	total				
	two week total				

28

Name _____

Food and diet

Family menu

	A menu for my family							
	Monday breakfast dinner tea	**Tuesday** breakfast dinner tea	**Wednesday** breakfast dinner tea	**Thursday** breakfast dinner tea	**Friday** breakfast dinner tea	**Saturday** breakfast dinner tea	**Sunday** breakfast dinner tea	
A menu for the Allen family	**Monday** breakfast dinner tea	**Tuesday** breakfast dinner tea	**Wednesday** breakfast dinner tea	**Thursday** breakfast dinner tea	**Friday** breakfast dinner tea	**Saturday** breakfast dinner tea	**Sunday** breakfast dinner tea	

Name _____

Escape from the workhouse: 1

❖ Can you help Mark and Anne escape from the workhouse? Read their story, then write your own ending. Is it happy or sad? You decide.

❖ Now look at the workhouse plan on Escape from the workhouse: 2. Draw and explain their escape route. What happens next?

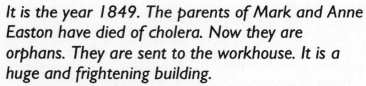

It is the year 1849. The parents of Mark and Anne Easton have died of cholera. Now they are orphans. They are sent to the workhouse. It is a huge and frightening building.

Mark and Anne have to wear a uniform. They are separated and made to sleep in wards with other boys and girls. Some of the other children are bullies.

The Master and Mistress, who run the workhouse, are not really cruel but they are too busy to worry about new children who are upset. The food is very plain, lots of gruel (thin porridge) and vegetables. They have to work every day picking oakum, that is slowly pulling apart old ropes from ships.

Each afternoon they have to go to lessons to read and write with Mr Thomas. He is an old teacher who lives in the workhouse because he can't look after himself any more.

One morning they are told that Anne is to be sent away to work as a kitchen maid in a big house in the town. They will hardly ever see each other. They decide to run away to 'Uncle Andrew' who works on a farm in the country, about 20 miles away. He is not a real uncle, but an old friend of their father's. They aren't sure if he will look after them but he is their only hope.

'Ticky Tom', who lives in the Idiot Ward, works in the garden and grows vegetables for the workhouse. He is not as daft as everyone believes. Tom has become their friend and wants to help.

Escape from the workhouse: 2

This is the ground floor plan of the workhouse where Mark and Anne have been sent. It holds 500 people.

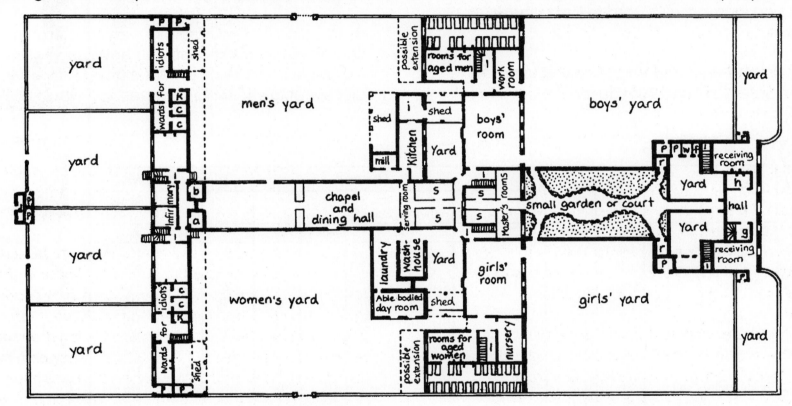

g stairs to the room where the guardians of the workhouse meet
f rooms for cleaning the clothes of the poor, ready to be given back to anyone who leaves
h the porter's room
w washing rooms

r lock-up room for trouble-makers
p toilets
s stores
i scullery
a surgery
b nurse's room

l stairs
d dead house
c cupboard
k storeroom

Eating in the workhouse

The chart below shows the food eaten each day by the men and women who used to live in the workhouse.

✤ What are the men and women given to eat for dinner on Saturdays and Tuesdays?

✤ List any good or bad points about this diet sheet.

✤ Imagine that you are the medical officer in charge of the workhouse and have been given the money to improve one meal a day. Draw up a new diet sheet to show the changes you would make.

		Breakfast		Dinner					Supper	
		bread	gruel	cooked meat	potatoes or other vegetables	soup	bread	cheese	bread	cheese
		oz	pints	oz	lb	pints	oz	oz	oz	oz
Sunday	men	8	1½				7	2	6	1½
	women	6	1½				6	1½	5	1½
Monday	men	8	1½				7	2	6	1½
	women	6	1½				6	1½	5	1½
Tuesday	men	8	1½	8	¾				6	1½
	women	6	1½	6	¾				5	1½
Wednesday	men	8	1½				7	2	6	1½
	women	6	1½				6	1½	5	1½
Thursday	men	8	1½			1½	6		6	1½
	women	6	1½			1½	5		5	1½
Friday	men	8	1½				7	2	6	1½
	women	6	1½				6	1½	5	1½
Saturday	men	8	1½	bacon 5	¾				6	1½
	women	6	1½	4	¾				5	1½

Name _____

What is my job?

♣ Look at the wordbox and match the job title with the correct picture.

♣ Now look at the advertisements on the Workshop of the world sheet. Which company do you think employed which worker?

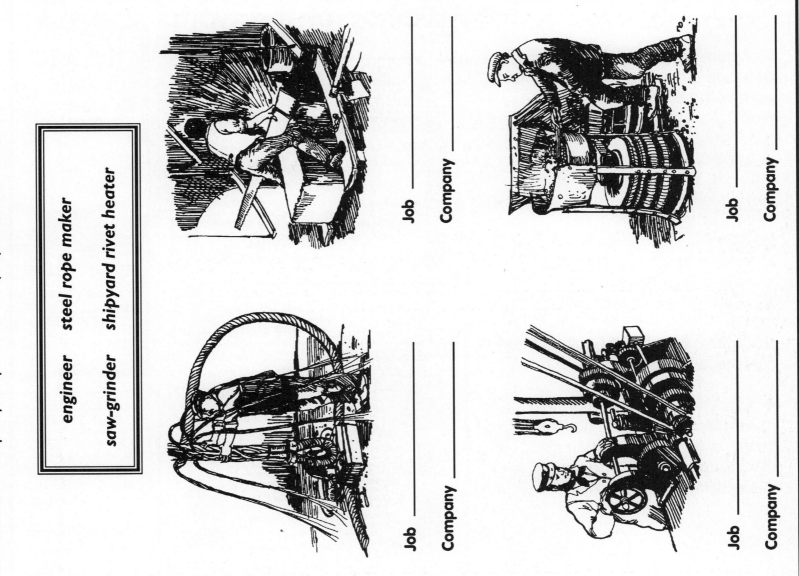

| *engineer* | *steel rope maker* |
| *saw-grinder* | *shipyard rivet heater* |

Job _____

Company _____

Job _____

Company _____

Job _____

Company _____

Job _____

Company _____

Name _____

Workshop of the world

Victorian industries sold so many goods to other countries that Britain earned the title 'Workshop of the world'.

✤ Look at the advertisements on the right. Which company would you go to if you:

• wanted to buy a saw;
• needed wire rope for a mine;
• wanted an engine for a crane;
• wanted to order a cargo ship?

✤ Make a list of all the things these companies made.

✤ Can you find anything in the advertisements which shows that these companies sold their goods in other countries? Why do you think this was important?

YORKSHIRE WIRE ROPE AND FENCING WORKS SHEFFIELD

JOHN SHAW, Jun.,
MANUFACTURER OF
STEEL AND IRON WIRE ROPES
FOR
COLLIERIES, RAILWAY INCLINES, STEAM CULTIVATORS
SHIPS' RIGGING, &c
Solid Copper Wire Rope Lightning Conductors.
COPPER WINDOW SASH CORD.
GILT & SILVER PICTURE CORD

BARTRAM AND SONS
SOUTH DOCK SUNDERLAND

HIGH CLASS CARGO STEAMER
FOR
THE EASTERN TRADE
OF WHICH THE FIRM HAVE BUILT SEVERAL

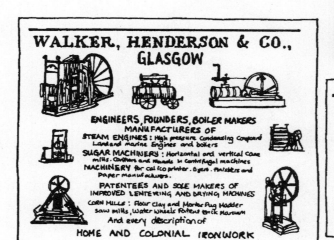

WALKER, HENDERSON & CO.,
GLASGOW

ENGINEERS, FOUNDERS, BOILER MAKERS
MANUFACTURERS OF
STEAM ENGINES : High pressure Condensing Compound Land and marine Engines and boilers
SUGAR MACHINERY : Horizontal and vertical Cane mills. Coolers and Rounds & Centrifugal machines
MACHINERY for calico printers. Dyers. Finishers and Paper manufacturers.
PATENTEES AND SOLE MAKERS OF
IMPROVED LENTERING AND DRYING MACHINES
CORN MILLS : Flour clay and Mortar Pug Madder saw mills, Water wheels Patent Brick Maroum
And every description of
HOME AND COLONIAL IRONWORK

CONSTANTINE BROTHERS
MERCHANTS AND MANUFACTURERS OF ALL KINDS OF
SAWS, FILES, STEEL,
SUITABLE FOR THE UNITED STATES, CANADIAN, THE BRITISH COLONIES AND CONTINENTAL MARKETS
CALICO WEBS, MACHINE KNIVES, BLADES, SPIRAL CUTTERS, &c.,

68 & 70, HOLLIS CROFT, SHEFFIELD

Name _____

Water power

Water wheels were the most important force used to drive machinery in factories. Steam engines did not replace them until after the 1820s. Water wheels could be built fairly easily, but steam engines needed an engineer to build them.

As the owner of a cotton mill you would have had the choice of two types of water wheel – overshot or undershot. In this activity you are going to make a water wheel and test the two types to see which turns faster.

overshot

undershot

❖ Make your own water wheel as shown in the diagram below.

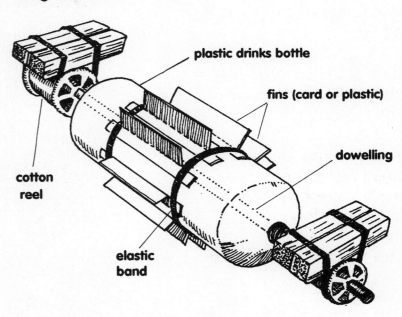

plastic drinks bottle

fins (card or plastic)

dowelling

cotton reel

elastic band

❖ Now use a shallow piece of guttering to guide water from a tap to the water wheel. Test your water wheel in the overshot and undershot positions. In which does the wheel turn faster? Why do you think this is so?

Name _____

Where should the factory be built?

♣ Imagine that you are Jebediah Strutt, a cotton cloth manufacturer. Your present mill is too small and you must choose a site to build a new one. Three possible places (sites A, B and C) are pointed out to you. Which would you choose? Why?

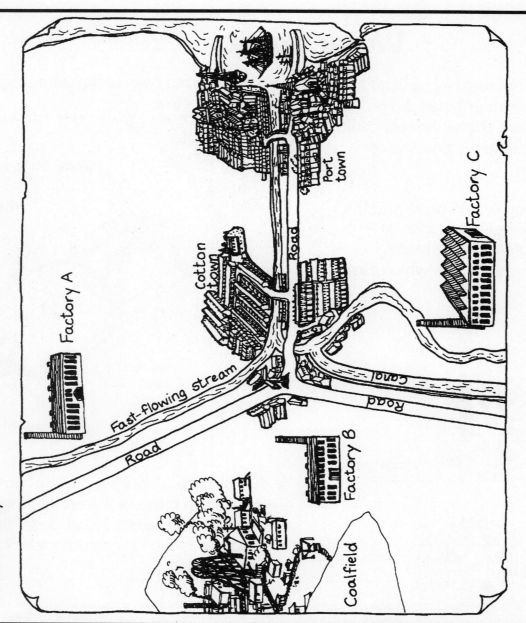

Factory A

Factory C

Port town

Cotton town

Road

Fast-flowing stream

Canal

Road

Road

Factory B

Coalfield

I chose site _____

because _____

♣ What sort of power do you want for your factory? What are its advantages and disadvantages?

_____

_____

36

Dangerous working conditions

Some people were worried about the conditions in the new factories. The workers toiled for many hours in the heat and noise. The machines they looked after did not have fences round them and could be dangerous.

In 1832 Parliament sent people called commissioners to investigate conditions inside the factories.

❖ Study the picture. If you had been a commissioner, what questions would you have asked the workers and factory owners?

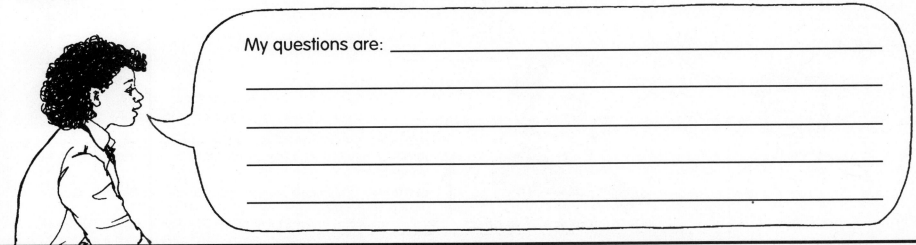

My questions are: _____

_____

_____

_____

_____

Name _____

Factory children

There were complaints of cruelty to children in the factories. Here is what some of the people involved had to say.

♣ Read what each person has to say, then write a sentence which begins:

I think _____ is to blame because ...

Thomas only told me once that he had been beaten. I told him not to mind and gave him a halfpenny. I found bruises on him and once he ran away. His father took his wages and we often gave him a penny to buy apples on Sunday.

Thomas Clarke's mother

I am aged eleven. I was a piecer for Joseph Badder, who used to beat me with a leather strap. Sometimes he hit me over the head when I fell asleep. But the factory owner's overseer was worse — he would strap me for no reason at all.

Thomas Clarke (piecer)

I have always found it difficult to keep my piecers awake the last hour of a working evening. I told the owner and he said I did not beat them enough. When the overseer, Thorpe, got into trouble for beating children the master always paid his fines.

Joseph Badder (chief spinner)

I have heard that men such as Badder punch the children and I do not think they need to do this. They should just speak very severely to them. Our last overseer, Thorpe, was bad tempered and I got rid of him.

The factory owner

piecer – had to mend any threads that broke when the cloth was being spun.
overseer – the factory owner used this man to see that work was done in his factory.

Children in the coal-mines

My name is Joseph Taylor. I work at Heaton Colliery, Northumberland. I am going on ten. I drive the rolleys, the coal wagons pulled by horses. I have been working for about nine months and get paid 1s 3d (6½p) a day.

Every morning I get up at three o'clock and start work in the pit at four o'clock. My first job is to light the candles and put them in the mistress. This is a small wooden box only open at one side. Next I fasten my horse to a train of three rolleys. Each rolley holds two corves, or big baskets of coal. I move the coal to a man called the onsetter. He works at the bottom of the shaft and sends the corves to the surface.

I go down the pit in an empty corve and have to hold on tight. I work until four o'clock in the afternoon. I eat my breakfast before I go. My bait is meat and bread. I eat them at ten and one o'clock or so. Sometimes I'm sleepy. Usually I fall off the rolleys at least once a day. Luckily I've never been hurt.

❖ Read the passage on this page.

❖ How old was Joseph?

_____

❖ Make a small picture dictionary to explain the following words: bait; corve; mistress; onsetter; rolley.

❖ Many people were shocked that children had to work in such conditions. What changes would you suggest to make their lives better?

Name _____

My daily routine

♣ Fill in the pie chart below to show what you do during a normal day. Use different colours to show how you spend your time.

♣ If there are other things you want to add use extra colours. Draw your own key to show what the colours mean.

red	at school
green	sleeping
yellow	playing
blue	watching TV
orange	eating

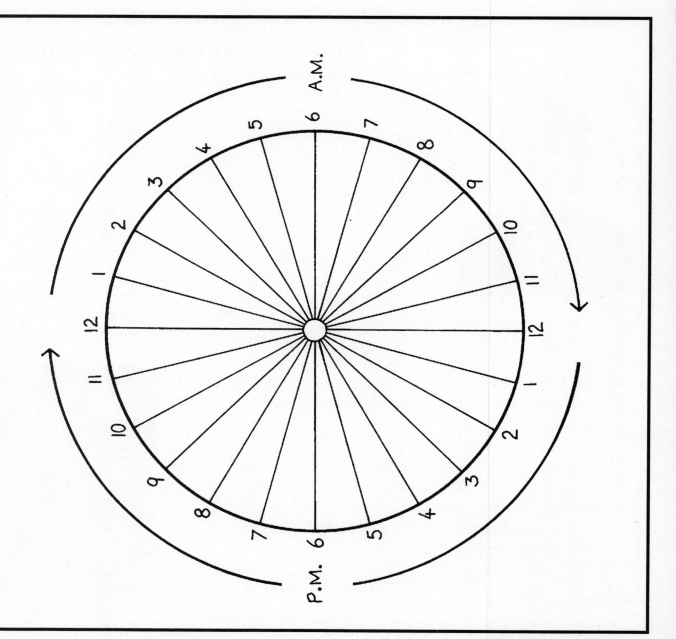

Name _____

Joseph Taylor's daily routine

❖ How did Joseph Taylor spend his day? (See the Children in the coal-mines sheet.)

You know how many hours he worked, but when and for how long would he have needed to sleep, eat and travel to work and back? Would he have had any time to play?

❖ Choose colours for each of the things Joseph did and fill in the key to show how your colour code works.

❖ Now colour in the pie chart.

key

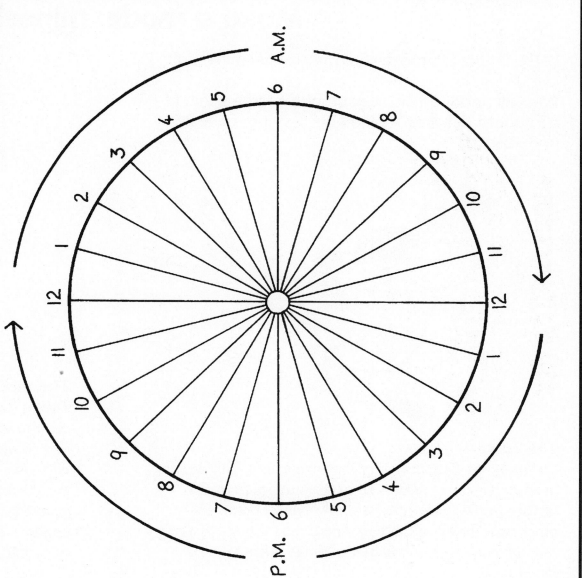

Coal mines

Make a model mineshaft: 1

You are going to make your own model mineshaft.

You will need: an old yoghurt pot; a large sheet of cardboard; a cotton reel; a pencil; string; adhesive and scissors.

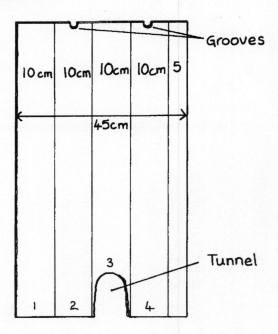

The corve
Cut away the bottom half of the yoghurt pot. This will be used as the corve, or basket, to carry things from the surface to the tunnel. Make small holes opposite each other near the lip of the pot, then thread a piece of string through each hole and knot it to make a loop.

The shaft
Take a long piece of cardboard (the longer the better) and cut it to 45cm in width. Draw lines to mark it off lengthways in four 10cm columns with a 5cm column at one edge. Cut a tunnel entrance at the bottom of one of the 10cm columns, then fold along the lines to make a square tube. Cut a small groove at the tops of two opposite columns and then glue the 'mineshaft' together using the 5cm strip.

Make a model mineshaft: 2

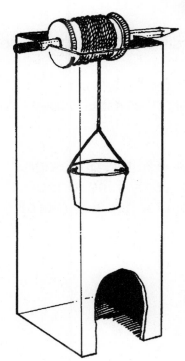

❖ Once you have completed your model, experiment to see how much weight it can carry by adding model miners made from Plasticine to the basket.

❖ Make a list of the dangers men faced underground when travelling like this.

❖ Imagine that you are the overman, or manager, of a coal mine. When your miners start work it is important to know who is going underground and when they return to the surface. Why would you need to know this and can you think of a way of keeping an exact check?

❖ Write a report together with any diagrams you think will be helpful to explain your plan.

The winding gear
Push a pencil or piece of dowel through the hole in the centre of the cotton reel. Tie one end of a long piece of string to the loop attached to the corve and wrap the rest around the cotton reel. Rest the pencil in the grooves at the top of the mineshaft so that the cotton reel is at the top of the mineshaft and the corve is hanging down inside. Lower the corve to the bottom of the shaft.

Name _____

Farming

A farm labourer's house

Most land in the countryside was owned by rich people. Those who worked for the rich on the farms were called 'labourers'. They lived in small cottages of stone with thatched roofs. The cottages were usually owned by the farmer.

✤ Look at this picture of a farm labourer's cottage.

✤ How many people are living in the house?

✤ How is the house different from the place in which you live?

✤ What is comfortable about this house? What is uncomfortable?

✤ Read the introduction to this page again. What would happen to this family if the farmer did not want the father to work for him any more?

The hiring fair

When farmers wanted to find workers for their farms, they went to the villages where a hiring fair was held. Farm workers would stand in the marketplace waiting to be offered work. At special times of the year farmers would choose the people they needed for their farms.

✤ The pictures below on the left show some of the things a farmer needs help with. The pictures on the right show some people who could be hired to do the different jobs on a farm.

✤ Match the people to the jobs.

Farming

The farming year

There was much work to be done on the farm. There were very few machines, and most of the work was done by hand or with the help of horses.

✤ Look at the pictures on this page. They each show a farm at different times of the year – winter, spring, summer and autumn. Which season does each of the pictures show?

✤ Cut the pictures out, then stick them in order on to paper and write the correct season name below each one.

Farm machinery

During Victorian times, the population of the country grew and more food was needed. As a result, farmers began to use machines to increase the amount of food they could produce.

✤ Compare the two pictures below.

✤ What differences can you see between the two pictures? How do you think these changes affected farming?

✤ Compare these pictures with methods of farming used today.

Washing clothes

Changing washday

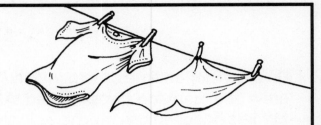

The pictures on this page show washday objects from Victorian times and today.

♣ Cut out the pictures and sort them into two groups – Victorian and modern.

♣ Now match each Victorian object with the modern-day object that does the same job.

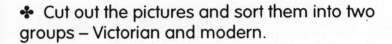

mangle

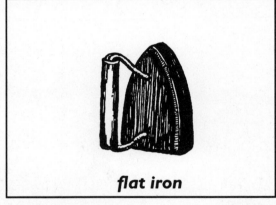

flat iron

spin dryer

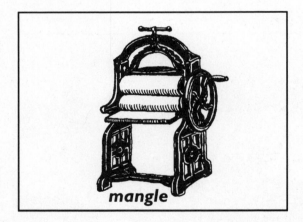

electric steam iron

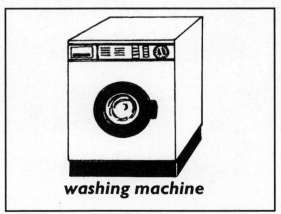

washing machine

poss tub and dolly

A housemaid's work

Most working women in Victorian Britain became housemaids. Here are some of the jobs that they had to do.

- clean out and blacklead (a kind of polish) the grates
- prepare and light the fires
- clean the fire-irons (poker, brush, pan, tongs)
- sweep the hearth
- polish the fenders
- dust the mantelpieces
- clean and trim the lamps (gas or oil)
- wash and polish the lamp glasses
- dust and clean the furniture
- sweep, wash and polish the linoleum (similar to floor tiles)
- sweep the carpets
- take the rugs and mats outside for beating
- clean the windows, pictures and mirrors
- clean the silverware, such as candlesticks, trays and teapots
- dust the skirting-boards and stairs
- air and make the beds

✤ Use the list of jobs to help you fill in the missing words on the picture below.

✤ Which jobs do not have to be done in modern houses? Why not?

✤ What would each of the fire-irons be used for?

✤ If most working women were servants, what does this tell us about the way women were treated in Victorian times?

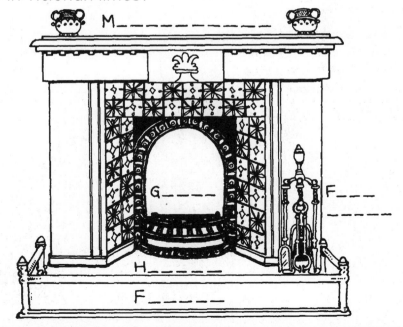

Working conditions

Strike!

Sometimes the factory owners and their workers could not agree, so the workers stopped work and went on strike.

♣ Look at the arguments shown here. Do you think they are fair? Underline what you think is a fact and what is a point of view.

You have bought new machines, so you must have a lot of money to pay us higher wages.

Henry Black – cotton worker

Last month you sold twice as much cotton cloth as the month before. You should pay us more wages.

Sally Blight – cotton worker

I cannot give you any more money. I can only sell my cotton cloth at half the price I used to! There are the new machines to pay for.

Mr Entwhistle – manager

I owe money to the bank for the new machines. I cannot pay you higher wages.

Mr Blunt – factory owner

Name _____

Trade unions

This picture is from a membership card for the Engineers' Trade Union.

AMALGAMATED SOCIETY OF ENGINEERS, MACHINISTS, MILLWRIGHTS SMITHS AND PATTERN MAKERS

♣ Find out what an engineer does.

♣ Look at the words in the ribbon at the bottom of the picture. Use a dictionary to find out the meaning of the words 'united' and 'industrious'. They will help you to understand the picture.

♣ What is there in the picture that tells you that the man who owned the membership card was an engineer?

♣ What is the man in the top left of the picture refusing? Why is this shown in the picture?

♣ Why is there an angel shown in the picture?

♣ What are the two men kneeling down trying to do? Why should this be shown in the picture?

There are three pictures of men inside three circles. The first man is James Watt, the second Archimedes (said Ark-im-eedees) and the third man Richard Arkwright. Find out what these people were famous for. Why would they be in this picture?

Trade union member

Here is a list of some early trade unions.

Amalgamated Society of Carpenters

Dock, Wharf, Riverside and General Labourers' Union

Matchmakers' Union

Gas Workers' Union

Boilermakers' Union

Union of Operative Spinners

Amalgamated Society of Locomotive Engineers and Firemen

Amalgamated Society of Railway Servants

Society of Milliners

Shoemakers' Society

Operative Stonemasons

✤ Choose one and draw a membership card for this union like the one on the Trade unions activity sheet. Include pictures and words that you think will show what your trade is and what your trade union believes in. Use reference books to help you.

Changes in the locality: 1

Maps are one of the best ways to find out about how a local area has changed over time.

✤ Look carefully at these two maps of a small part of Sunderland. The map on this sheet is dated 1856 and the map on sheet 2 1896.

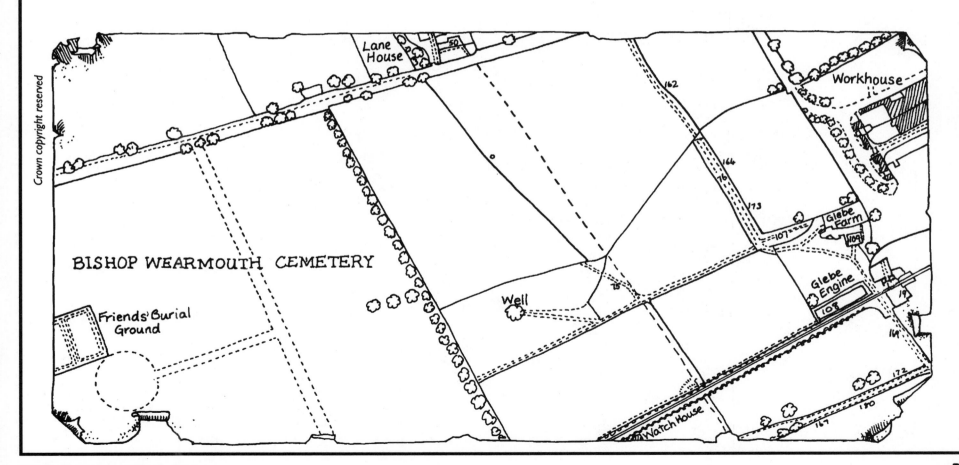

Crown copyright reserved

Lane House

Workhouse

Glebe Farm

BISHOP WEARMOUTH CEMETERY

Well

Glebe Engine

Friends' Burial Ground

Watch House

Changes in the locality: 2

✤ How many years after map 1 was map 2 made?

✤ On another piece of paper make two lists showing:

- things that have changed between 1856 and 1896;
- things that have stayed the same.

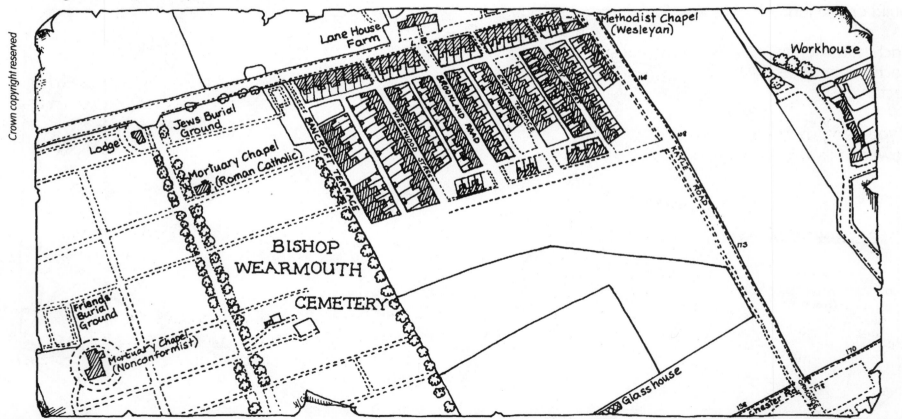

Back to back housing: 1

Back to back housing was very cheap to build. There were no back lanes between adjoining houses, and most houses had no tap water, drains or sewers.

♣ Imagine that you have bought a piece of land to build houses for workers. The more houses you can build on the land, the greater the profit you can make.

Each house on the plan should measure 4cm x 2cm. Each house costs £20 to build. Draw them as rectangles.

If you add pavements, tap water and drains and sewers, this will make the houses more expensive.

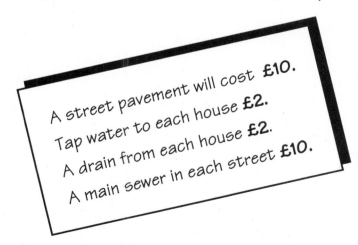

A street pavement will cost £10.
Tap water to each house £2.
A drain from each house £2.
A main sewer in each street £10.

♣ Draw your houses on the plan on Back to back housing: 2 and include any other features, such as tap water and so on, using the key below.

> **D** = drain   **T** = tap water
>
> **S** = main sewer   **P** = pavement

♣ Add up the cost of your houses. Compare your costs with other people in the class. Explain why your houses were cheaper or more expensive than others.

Name _____

Houses

Back to back housing: 2

Use this sheet with Back to back housing: 1.

Which house do you like?

Many Victorian houses are still in use today.

✤ Look carefully at these two pictures of the same terraced house – one showing how it looked in 1886 and the other as it is today.

✤ What has changed? Why do you think these changes have happened?

✤ Do you think the house looks better now or as it was in 1886? Give your reasons.

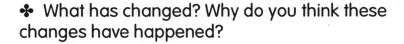

1886

today

Houses

Slum conditions

Read through the following extract which comes from a Report on the Sanitary Conditions of Newcastle, Gateshead, North Shields, Sunderland, Durham and Carlisle (1845) by Dr D.B. Reid.

The street where the poorest people live is full of filth where the sun never reaches...

Next to the houses were some piggeries which gave off a dreadful smell. Added to this are long open sewers which cross the paths.

In most cases whole families share one room and lodging houses [very cheap hotels] are badly crowded with little fresh air. Sometimes two people sleep in the bed — one at night and the other during the day.

Dense black clouds of smoke pour out from the factories and as much as 20-30 tons of acid fall from this smoke on to this part of the town.

❧ Imagine that the town council have asked you to tell them what must be done to clean up this part of town.

Begin your report:

I recommend that the town council should:

_____

_____

signed (your name) _____

Cholera

During Victorian times many people lived in very dirty and unhealthy houses. These people were likely to catch diseases and die. One of the worst diseases was called cholera (said col-er-a). It killed many people who lived in unhealthy conditions.

♣ Imagine you are a doctor living today. How have things changed since the time of Victoria? Draw pictures in the empty boxes to show how things are today.

then	now
 There was no running water for each house.	
The whole street often shared one toilet.	
 Many families only had one room to live in.	

Disease

Burying the victims: 1

Burying the victims: 2 shows a parish register of all the people who died in one area of Newcastle when cholera was at its worst.

✤ Count up the numbers of people who died each week.

✤ Count up the number of people who died of cholera in December.

✤ Draw a column graph showing the number of people who died each week and how many of them died of cholera. For example:

✤ In which week did most people die?

_____

✤ At what age did most people die of the disease?

_____

✤ Is this evidence enough to tell you how people died of cholera? What other things would you need to know?

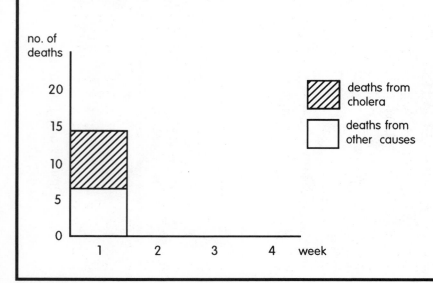

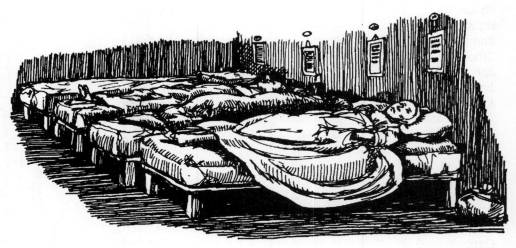

Burying the victims: 2

Name	When buried	Age	Cause of death	Name	When buried	Age	Cause of death
1831				James Thompson	Dec 22	–	cholera
John Graham Fenwick	Dec 2 Fri	9 weeks		Mary Muffatee	Dec 22	36 years	cholera
Jane Bell	Dec 5	79 years		Thomas Jolling	Dec 22	28 years	cholera
Elizabeth Miller	Dec 4	17 years		Elizabeth Clint	Dec 23 Fri	50 years	cholera
Elizabeth Hedley	Dec 4	61 years		Ann Wailes	Dec 23	35 years	cholera
Joseph Miller	Dec 5	9 days		Mary Charlton	Dec 23	2 weeks	
Richard Cooper	Dec 7	1½ years		William McLaughlin	Dec 23	70 years	cholera
Mary Marchbank	Dec 9 Fri	75 years	cholera	Elizabeth McConnic	Dec 24	5 years	
Ann Dixon	Dec 9	27 years		Elizabeth Richardson	Dec 24	22 years	cholera
Elizabeth Richardson	Dec 10	77 years	cholera	Ann Wilkinson	Dec 24	49 years	cholera
Jane Cadwallader	Dec 11	13 years		Esther Smith	Dec 25	40 years	cholera
Isaac Wailes	Dec 12	23 years	cholera	Jane Davison	Dec 25	45 years	cholera
Margaret Dodds	Dec 12	11 years		Ann Orrick	Dec 25	31 years	
Helen McDonald	Dec 12	25 years	cholera	Winifred Hines	Dec 26	67 years	
Isabella Pybus	Dec 13	91 years		Elizabeth Mooney	Dec 26	75 years	
James Robson	Dec 13	14 days		Robert Dickinson	Dec 26	35 years	cholera
William Clark	Dec 13	40 years		Jane Bell	Dec 27	72 years	cholera
Elizabeth Ridley	Dec 13	70 years	cholera	Margaret Forsyth	Dec 28	11 years	cholera
Ann Carrick	Dec 15	50 years		George Pinkerton	Dec 28	85 years	cholera
Grace Leonard	Dec 15	6 years	cholera	Isabella Peacock	Dec 28	56 years	cholera
Ann Clarke	Dec 15	35 years	cholera	Martha Elliott	Dec 28	40 years	cholera
Jane Scott	Dec 15	54 years	cholera	Ann Sloan	Dec 29	45 years	cholera
John Ridley	Dec 15	39 years	cholera	Mary Ann Jones	Dec 29	14 years	cholera
Thomas Ridley	Dec 15	2½ years	cholera	Elizabeth Hunter	Dec 29	36 years	cholera
Isabella Hidley	Dec 16 Fri	35 years	cholera	Peter Keevins	Dec 29	28 years	cholera
Elizabeth Mewing(?)	Dec 17	58 years	cholera	Richard Urwin	Dec 30 Fri	40 years	cholera
Peter Leonard	Dec 17	3 years	cholera	Mary Dixon	Dec 30	48 years	cholera
Mary Jackson	Dec 18	85 years		Elizabeth Heslop	Dec 30	78 years	suspicious
Ann Donnison	Dec 18	25 years	suspicious	Elizabeth Young	Dec 30	26 years	cholera
William Smith	Dec 19	72 years		Eleanor Laslie	Dec 31	50 years	cholera
Mary Smith	Dec 20	45 years	cholera	Elizabeth Watson	Dec 31	10 months	cholera
Elizabeth Walker	Dec 21	–	cholera	Mary Noble	Dec 31	34 years	cholera
Ann Anderson	Dec 21	47 years	cholera	Jane Summerbell	Dec 31	65 years	cholera
(?)Hanncell Dantze	Dec 21	–					

Shops

Make a Victorian shopping street: 1

✤ Below is a typical Victorian shop. Invent some shops of your own and complete the other drawings on these pages. Fill in:

- *the shop's name;*
- *the goods you are selling;*
- *the shop sign.*

✤ Carefully colour in the shops and place them next to your friends' shops to make a 'street'. Cut them out and join them together so that the chimneys match.

J.D. CASSELS.

HOSIER   MERCER

CLOTHIER   HATTER

Make a Victorian shopping street: 2

✤ Use this sheet with Make a Victorian shopping street: 1.

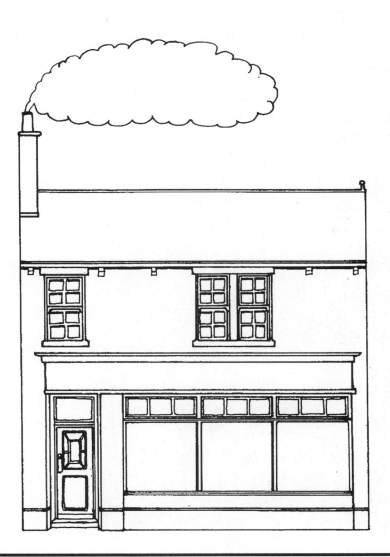

Name _____

Hygiene

Trouble with toilets

Is your toilet comfortable? Is it in a warm clean bathroom? Then think about this.

Most Victorian toilets were ash closets at the bottom of the back yard. They weren't flushed with running water. When someone went to the toilet they sprinkled ashes on top. Once a week men called 'scavengers' came round and emptied the dirty ashes. This wasn't very healthy and caused a lot of disease, especially among children.

❖ Draw a picture of a modern bathroom in the space provided below.

❖ Can you find three differences between the ash closet and the modern toilet?

Spotting Victorian street names

Many of the street names in use today are from Victorian times.

Politicians
Beaconsfield or Disraeli Street – Conservative Prime Minister, 1874–1880.
Gladstone Street – Liberal Prime Minister three times.

The Royal family
Victoria Street – Queen from 1837 to 1901.
Albert Street – Victoria's husband, died 1861.
Coronation Street – Victoria was crowned in 1837.

Scientists, inventors and engineers
Faraday Street – inventor of the electric motor.
Swan Street – inventor of the electric light bulb.

Generals
Cardigan Street – Commander of the Light Brigade in the Crimean War.
Havelock Street – hero of the Indian mutiny.

Writers
Brontë Street – three sisters, Anne, Charlotte and Emily.
Dickens Street – author of *Oliver Twist*.

Wars and battles
Lucknow Street – Lucknow was a city in India which was besieged during the Indian mutiny.
Mafeking Street and Ladysmith Street – cities attacked during the Boer War, 1899–1902.

Countries and cities of the Empire
Australia Street, Sydney Street, Melbourne Street.
Kenya Street, Nairobi Street.

♣ Use an A–Z street atlas to check if any of these names are used in your local area. Make a list of the ones you can find. (Remember to check other words for street, such as Road or Terrace.)

♣ Choose one of the famous names listed here and find out what you can about that person or place.

♣ With the help of your local studies library or archives, find out if any other streets near you are named after Victorian people, places or events. Some names may only be well known in your area.

Name _____

Street furniture

Street furniture

Street furniture is the name given to large man-made objects found in the street which are usually there to help people.

❖ Look at the pictures below. Match each one with the correct name in the wordbox.

❖ Explain how each piece of Victorian street furniture was useful.

| gas lamp | tram wire post | shop awning | iron railings |

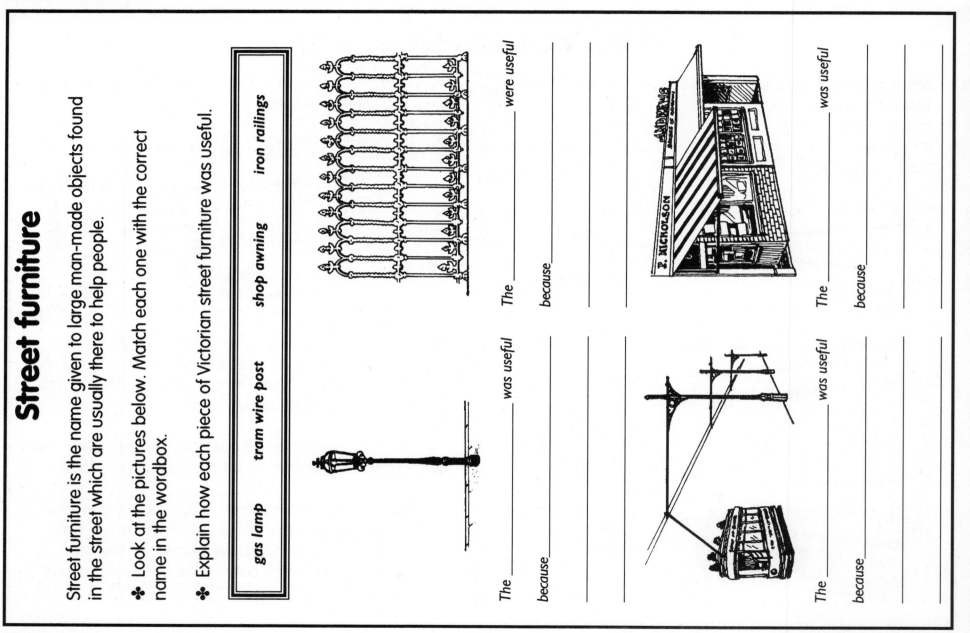

The _____ were useful

because _____

The _____ was useful

because _____

The _____ was useful

because _____

The _____ was useful

because _____

Who lived or worked here?

Street directories were like a Victorian version of the *Yellow Pages*. Sometimes they listed people in alphabetical order like a phone book, sometimes they listed them street by street. The example on this page is taken from a Belfast street directory from 1877.

♣ Where would you go for the following on Castle Lane:
- to have a meal?
- to stay the night?

♣ What kinds of buildings are there on Castle Lane besides shops?

♣ Can you tell if Castle Lane is a rich or poor street?

♣ Choose a Victorian street near your school. Go to your local studies library or record office and check the local street directories. How is your street similar to, or different from, Castle Lane?

Castle Lane

Arthur Square to Donegall Place

1   Gelston, Joseph, manufacturing jeweller
3   Silo, George L., tobacconist.
    Burnstein, Murray & Co., cigarette manufacturers.
5   Rankin Bros., watchmakers, jewellers, and opticians.
5   Durand, A., hairdressser and perfumer, and shampooing rooms (first floor).
7   Thomas, Philip W., district manager, Great Britain Fire Insurance Co. and Great Britain Mutual Assurance Society.
9 & 11   Abercorn Arms Hotel – Miss Johnston, proprietress.
13 Hanson, John, land agent.
15 Ranagan, B., ladies' and gentlemen's hairdresser, wig maker and ladies' head dress manufacturer, and shampooing rooms.
17 Gibson, John, bookseller.
19 Wellington Arms Hotel – Andrew Majury, proprietor.
21 & 23   Mitchell, Mrs John, fishmonger.
25 Boyd, John, nursery and seedsman.

27 Kerr, Alex., meal[1] & flourdealer.
29 Rice, E., meal and flourdealer.
31 Castle Restaurant and Luncheon Bar – George Fisher, proprietor.
33 Neill, James, & Co., jewellers – side entrance.
14 Imperial Hotel - back entrance.
12½ Crawford & Sons, J., bonded[2] stores.
... *Calender Street intersects*
12 Murtagh, Thos., spirit dealer.
8 & 10   Ulster Restaurant and Luncheon Bar – John Wilson, proprietor.
6   Kennedy, Joseph, tobacconist.
4   Carroll, Mrs and Miss, ladies' underclothing and baby linen warehouse.
2   Theatre Royal – side entrance.

1 meal means oatmeal, used to make porridge.
2 bonded means goods on which customs duties have to be paid.

Buildings

Name _____

Then and now

This Victorian school is built of stone, with a black slate roof. It is one storey high, with nine classrooms.

✤ Look carefully at this picture. Find as many differences as you can between the outside of this school and your own.

✤ Imagine that you travel back in time to go to this school in 1870. Describe one thing you would like about the building and one thing you would dislike.

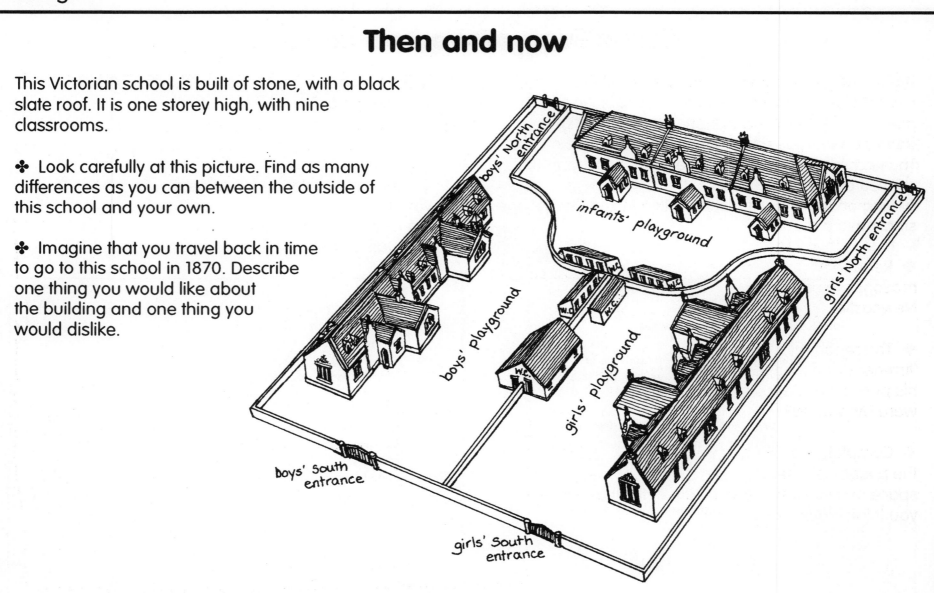

boys' North entrance

infants' playground

girls' North entrance

boys' playground

girls' playground

W.C.

Boys' South entrance

girls' South entrance

Going to the Ragged School: 1

When Victoria became Queen many children did not go to school, and those that did had to pay. In 1844, the Ragged School Union was set up to provide free schools for the very poor. These children were often neglected, half-starved and dressed in rags. Many had to earn a living on the streets, sometimes by begging or stealing.

✤ Read the extract on sheet 2. Give two reasons why a Ragged School was set up in Newcastle.

✤ The report tells us that Mr Murray used 'firmness and kindness' to gain the respect of his pupils. What would you have done if you were Mr Murray?

✤ Complete the newspaper advertisement for the post of teacher to replace Mr Murray in the space on the right. Describe the kind of person you think would be needed.

WANTED BY:
NEWCASTLE UPON TYNE RAGGED SCHOOL –
an intelligent and devoted teacher. He must be able to offer the following qualities:

Going to the Ragged School: 2

This extract is taken from the 'First Report of the Newcastle upon Tyne Ragged School', 1848.

For a long time crime caused by children has been a problem. Since it is difficult to offer proper training to the very poor who are not in the workhouse, some friends of education in this town decided to set up a Ragged School in Newcastle. This was opened in Sandgate, a most wretched locality. Within a few days nearly 40 boys were attending.

The master, James Murray, had for many years been a Sunday school teacher. He used both firmness and kindness to change the unruly conduct of the boys. To stop them returning to begging or stealing it was necessary to offer each child a pennyworth of bread and cheese daily.

Sadly we must report that last winter an awful fever raged through this town, particularly in Sandgate. Many of the children fell ill, though only one died. Mr Murray, who had visited many of his pupils, was at length struck down. He died leaving a widow and child.

After a short time a new school room was obtained in Gibson Street, on higher and more healthy ground. The number of pupils now on the books is 45. Twelve have lost a father and eight a mother. Most of them come from miserable homes where they live in ignorance.

Punish the child

Each of these pupils has done something wrong. Imagine you are the teacher of this class. Look at the list on the right. How would you punish the child in each case? Write the letter in the box next to each name to show the punishment you have chosen.

a) not punish the child;
b) send a letter home;
c) give them the cane (how many strokes?);
d) keep them behind after school;
e) other?

☐ *Jane Luxton has failed to form the letter 's' properly in writing practice.*

☐ *Brian Smith has broken a steel pen nib in writing practice.*

☐ *Ann Noble has not got the penny fee for school. Both her parents are out of work.*

☐ *John Tackworth has had a fight with Samuel Sneck over name-calling.*

☐ *Peter Raston has been off school for two days to help his parents with the harvest.*

☐ *Prudence Kickton has stolen a marble from David Elton.*

School fees

Name _____

Problem child

Tom had been given a penny by his parents to give to the schoolmaster, Mr Clarkson. Schooling wasn't free. It had to be paid for by the long hours Tom's dad bent over the power loom in the mill until his back ached and the day grew dark. It was also paid for by Tom's mother, whose nimble fingers changed the bobbins and twisted the thread together to keep the looms turning.

Passing Mr Doulberry's sweet shop Tom noticed the bull's-eye sweets winking at him and the candy sticks glistening in the window.

Before he knew it the sweets and the penny were gone.

♣ What did Tom do next? Finish off the story.

- Does Tom go into school?
- What happens to him if he does?
- Does Tom decide not to go to school that day?
- What happens when his parents find out?

Dressing for school

These pictures show how children used to dress for school in Victorian times.

♣ Look carefully at the pictures and make a list of the similarities and differences between the way

children used to dress for school and the way you dress today.

♣ What do you like/dislike about the Victorian children's clothing?

Boys and girls

Educating girls

✤ Read the advertisements for schools on this page. They are both dated 1838. Do you think this education was for rich or poor people?

✤ What are the differences between what the girls and the boys were taught? Why do you think there were these differences?

✤ Why do you think people at this time did not consider it important to educate working people?

✤ Now look at the picture, which is based on a photograph of two girls at school in 1890.

- What are the girls learning to do?
- Are they likely to be from rich or poor homes?
- Why would girls be taught this sort of work?
- Does this suggest that education for girls has improved since 1838?
- What might poorer boys be learning?

Young men are carefully instructed in the English, Latin and Greek languages, writing, arithmetic, keeping money records, measuring, surveying, geometry, geography and navigation at £21 per year.

A School for Young Ladies within two miles of Hyde Park, London. The cost will be £21 per year. This will include instruction in English and French languages, writing and arithmetic, geography and history, playing the piano, singing and dancing.

Folding and mangling

The Inspector's visit

Every school that wanted a grant towards its upkeep was visited by one of Her Majesty's Inspectors. Once a year they checked on standards of teaching and learning. If the children did not come up to the expected standard the school might not have received its grant – and the teachers might not have been paid! Everyone had to be on their best behaviour on the day of the inspection.

On the right are three thoughts.

a) *'The handwriting of these children is very poor. They use slates too much and have not had enough practice with pen and ink.'*

b) *'He's not looking very pleased. What am I going to say to the headmaster if he complains?'*

c) *'I like Miss Thompson. She is a kind teacher who makes us laugh. I wish this horrible man would stop frightening her.'*

❖ Who do you think was thinking these things? Match each statement with one of the people below. Write 'a', 'b' or 'c' in the boxes to show your answers.

☐ **teacher**

☐ **inspector**

☐ **pupil**

❖ What will the Inspector say to Miss Thompson before he leaves? What will she say in reply?

❖ Explore this situation through role-play.

Prepare a lesson

Victorian teachers taught 'object lessons' to the youngest children in school. These lessons involved learning facts about a particular subject and included writing, talking and drawing. If possible, the teacher would bring the 'object' into the classroom. If not, the lesson was based around a large picture chart.

✤ The 'object lessons' listed below were taught at a school in 1898. Choose one and prepare a short lesson on it for your class. This should include ten quick facts about your object and a picture chart.

✤ How many of these subjects are still taught today? Are they taught in the same way?

Syllabus of work for the year ending May 31, 1898

1 The farmyard
2 Spring
3 Summer
4 Autumn
5 Winter
6 Birds
7 The mine
8 Fish
9 Wheat
10 The potato
11 The oak tree
12 The apple tree
13 The spider and his web
14 The butterfly
15 A newspaper
16 A frog

17 The railway
18 The buttercup
19 Sponges
20 The Queen and the Union Jack
21 Things that dissolve – sugar, salt, etc
22 Oranges
23 Tea
24 Coffee
25 Cocoa
26 The horse
27 Rabbits
28 Honey and its value
29 Fowls
30 The pig
31 Lead pencils
32 Matches

Pounds, shillings and pence

Victorian money was different from the money we use today. They used £...s...d.

£ = *pounds*
s = *shillings*
d = *pence*

This is how their money worked:

12 pence = *I shilling*
20 shillings = *I pound*

These drawings show both sides of different Victorian coins.

♣ Cut circles from card the same size as these coin drawings. Then stick the drawings to each side of the card circles to make pretend coins.

♣ Work together with your friends to play money counting games.

sovereign
(a £1 coin)

shilling

penny

halfpenny

Name _____

Lessons

Recitation: 1

English lessons in Victorian schools included learning passages of poetry by heart. Pupils then said them out loud, showing feeling and sympathy for what the poem was about. This poem comes from a book called *Historical Ballads* published in the 1880s. It was thought to be suitable for a 'moderately intelligent and well taught child of nine'.

 **Victoria's Promise**
by C.J. Coleridge (*About 1835*)

[1] Near London is a garden,
All fresh and green and cool,
Where little children run and laugh,
And ducks swim in a pool.

[2] The children feed the ducklings,
Birds sing and all is gay,
Near to the fine old palace,
At the blooming of the May.

[3] Within that old red palace,[1]
One morning long ago,
A maiden said her lessons,
And learnt to read and sew.

[4] A stately little lady –
Blue-eyed and fair to see,
With all her might and all her wits,
She learned her history...

[5] 'See, princess,' said her tutor,
'The root from which you spring,
Shew how the throne descended
To our present gracious King.'

[6] Through Saxon, Dane and Norman,
Through good and ill report,
From Egbert down to William,
The royal line she sought.

[7] Plantagenet and Tudor,
Scotch Stuart and German Guelph,
Down all the generations,
At last she found herself.

[8] 'My uncle has no children,
Who, when he comes to die,
Will then be King of England –
Oh, mother – is it I?...

[9] 'My child,' then said her mother,
'You are King William's heir,
You will be Queen of England,
God keep you in His care!'

[10] And then the child's white forehead
Flushed with new thoughts and fears;
Her blue eyes shone with purpose,
Although they filled with tears...

[11] She has had many troubles,
She has wept bitter tears,
She has borne many burdens,
She has lived many years.

[12] But she has kept her promise
Through all her length of life,
And all her subjects bless her –
Good mother, Queen, and wife.

1 Kensington Palace

Recitation: 2

♣ Read the poem on sheet 1. How much can you learn by heart? Practise by working in small groups and taking turns to say a verse.

♣ What do you think the poem is about?

♣ Copy out verses 10 and 11 of the poem in the box on the right. In the space below write instructions to tell the reader how to say the poem out loud. Tell them what feelings to use in their voice.

♣ Underline any words in the poem that you do not understand. Do you think this poem is easy to read? What does this tell you about Victorian schoolchildren?

Name _____

Lessons

Handwriting practice

Can you write as neatly as a Victorian child?

✤ Using the blank practice lines copy these sentences as carefully as you can. Remember every letter must be in the right place. If you get it wrong – do it again!

✤ Why do you think these sentences were chosen for the children to copy?

Keep not what is not your own.

Live peaceably with all men.

Changes in transport 1840–1900

There were many developments in transport during the reign of Queen Victoria. Steam ships replaced sailing ships. Cars replaced the horse and carriage and a new form of transport – railways – appeared.

❖ Cut out the pictures on this page and then sort them into pairs according to the form of transport

that they show. Look at each pair and place the earlier one first. What differences can you see between them? Write down your answers for each pair.

❖ Do you think the ways they have changed are for the better or for the worse?

Name _____

Carrying goods

Which form of travel?

In the nineteenth century there were several ways in which goods were carried around the country.

✤ Look at the pictures on this page. In the box next to each picture, note down the advantages and disadvantages of that form of travel.

Travel by road

At the beginning of the Victorian period, travel by road was slow and difficult.

❖ Read what each traveller has written about in the extracts. What are the differences between these descriptions?

❖ Now compare the two pictures. Why might these people have different things to say about their travels?

It was a very cold evening and the poor passengers on the top suffered greatly. When the coach finally got to the city it was discovered that one of the passengers riding on top had frozen to death.

From From York to London by Coach (1834)

Nothing more miserable and chilling can be imagined than travelling by coach. At the start of daybreak on a cold frosty morning, the roads are hard and slippery and the cold gets through to our bones.

From a private diary written by John Cabbell (1833)

When we leave the town behind on a bright summer's day we are dashing along the open road. The fresh air is blowing in our faces and our hearts are bursting with joy.

From Pickwick Papers by Charles Dickens (1837)

By road

Getting faster

✤ Look at this list of timings for stage and mail coach journeys to or from London. What does this tell you about changes in stage coach travel over the years? Write your ideas in the space on the right.

1658	Exeter (274km) 4 days
1706	York (336km) 4 days
1754	Edinburgh (652km) 11 days; Manchester (320km) 4½ days
1757	Liverpool (338km) 3 days
1784	Edinburgh 2½ days
1797	Exeter 25 hours
1825	Edinburgh 43 hours; Liverpool 27 hours
1836	Exeter 17 hours; Manchester 19 hours; Holyhead (430km) 27 hours

✤ Can you find out how long it takes to travel these distances by road today?

Canals: advantages

✤ Look at this collection of evidence and list all the advantages of canals.

Source A

The Aire Canal gives an easy way to connect the salt mines of Cheshire, the pottery makers of Staffordshire, coal from Derbyshire and farming produce from Leicestershire and Lincolnshire.

Joseph Priestley (1831)

Source C

These costs for carrying coal from Wedgwood's pottery works to Manchester were calculated in 1792 (they have been converted to modern currency).

Cost of carrying goods (per ton)

canal	road
75p	£2.75

Source B

In about 1800 a group of engineers carried out some experiments to see what load a horse could carry using different forms of transport. Here are the results:

		tons
1	Pack horse	$\frac{1}{8}$
2	Stage wagon, soft road	$\frac{5}{8}$
3	Stage wagon, Macadam road	2
4	Barge on river	30
5	Barge on canal	50
6	Wagon on iron rails	8

Source D

This is a picture of Josiah Wedgwood's pottery works.

Canals: disadvantages

✤ Look at this collection of evidence and list all the disadvantages of canals.

Source A
To make it possible for barges to travel uphill, or downhill, locks were built. Below is a diagram of how a lock works.

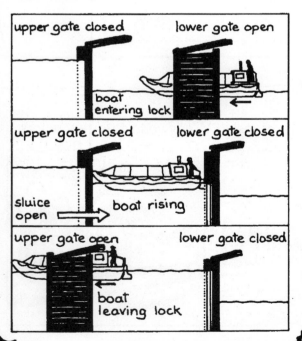

Source B
This chart shows the number of days the Stroudwater–Berkeley Canal was closed.

year	by frost	for repairs	by other causes	total
1809	21	16	14 (Thames floods)	51
1822	0	127	-	127
1826	20	26	70 (Stroudwater – Berkeley Canal junction)	116
1827	19	39	-	58
1828	0	40	-	40
1829	4	63 (tunnel)	-	67
1830	40	5	35 (Stroudwater repairs)	80
1839	0	28	-	28

Source C
Movement was slow on the canals. There were queues at the entrances to locks and tunnels. Most barges could travel no faster than two–three miles per hour.
From *A Historical Account of the Navigable Rivers, Canals and Railways throughout Great Britain* (1831)

Railways: for and against

❖ All of the things on this page tell us something about the early railways.

❖ Imagine that you were alive during Victorian times. Write a postcard to your grandchildren about what you expect your first railway journey to be like.

❖ On the back of this sheet, write a letter to someone who has never been on a train journey explaining all the good things railways will bring.

*When it's finished at both ends
You may send your cocks and hens
And go and visit all your friends
With ducks and pigs and turkeys.
To any part wherever you please
You may send your butter and eggs
And they can ride who've got no legs
Along the Oxford Railway.*

The Oxford Railway Song (1852)

There were thousands of people who said they would never put a foot in a railway carriage. *A few of them never did. My stepmother on her first railway journey pressed her handkerchief tightly to her eyes and begged not to look. She was a picture of terror.*

Sir J. Macdonald writing about early rail travel

Railroad travelling is the best improvement of human life. Man is free as a bird.

Written by *the Reverend Sydney Smith* (1842)

What will become of the coach makers, inn keepers and the beauty of the countryside? Smoke will kill the birds as they fly over the locomotive (train). The sparks from the chimney will burn the countryside. Elderly people feel they will be run over. Ladies will be upset that their horses would take fright. Cows will stop giving milk.

From The History of the English Railway J. Francis (1851)

Railways

Race against time

Play this game with a partner.

You will need: a coin and two counters.

✤ Toss a coin to decide who will be the stage coach company and who the railway company.

✤ Take it in turns to spin the coin and move your counter along the track. Heads means you can move two spaces, tails one space.

✤ Who finishes the journey from Cardiff to Swansea first?

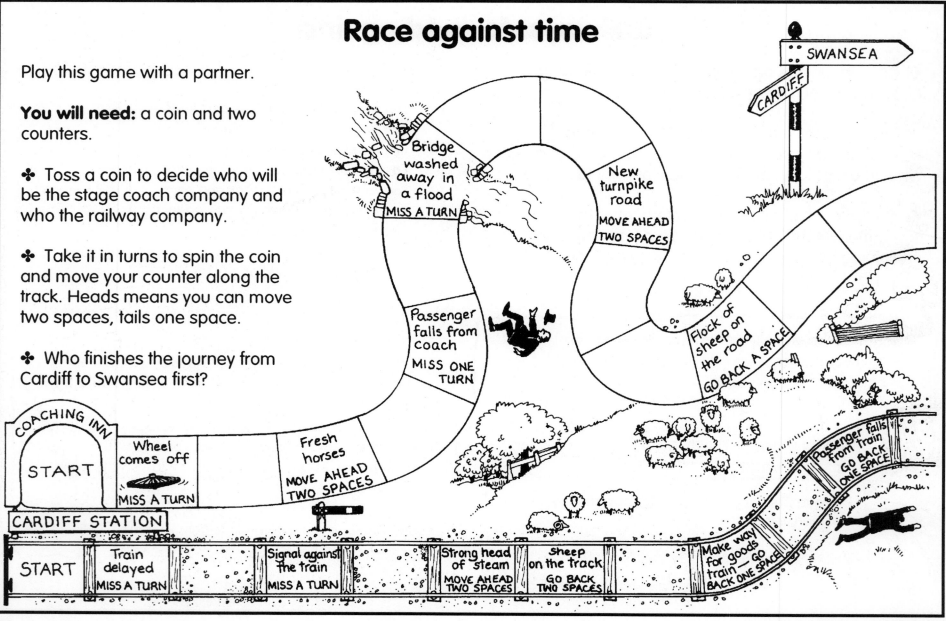

SWANSEA

CARDIFF

Bridge washed away in a flood
MISS A TURN

New turnpike road
MOVE AHEAD TWO SPACES

Passenger falls from coach
MISS ONE TURN

Flock of sheep on the road
GO BACK A SPACE

COACHING INN
START

Wheel comes off
MISS A TURN

Fresh horses
MOVE AHEAD TWO SPACES

Passenger falls from train
GO BACK ONE SPACE

CARDIFF STATION

START

Train delayed
MISS A TURN

Signal against the train
MISS A TURN

Strong head of steam
MOVE AHEAD TWO SPACES

Sheep on the track
GO BACK TWO SPACES

Make way for goods train — GO BACK ONE SPACE

Name _____

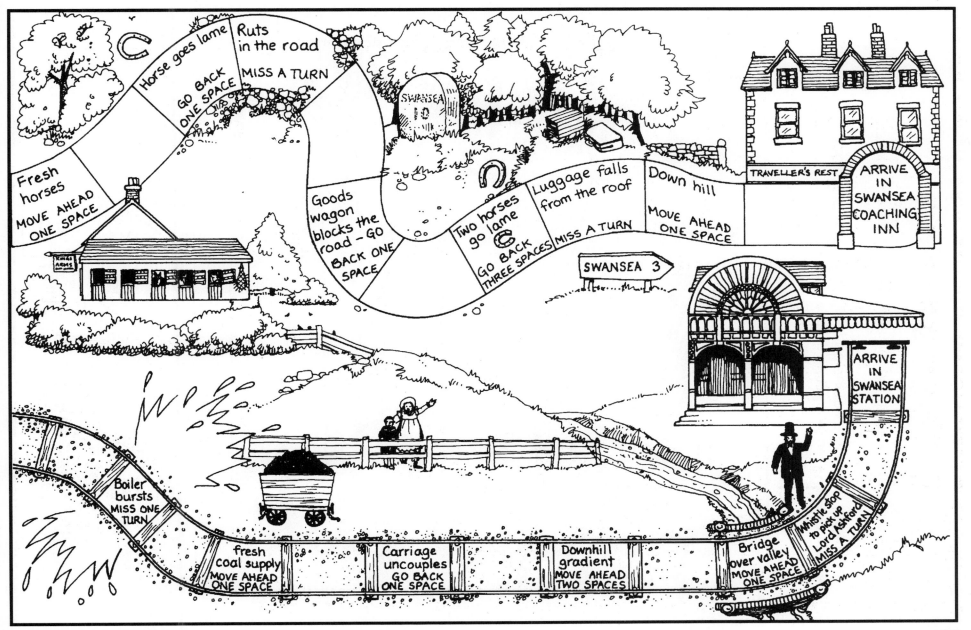

Horse goes lame
GO BACK ONE SPACE

Ruts in the road
MISS A TURN

SWANSEA 10

Fresh horses
MOVE AHEAD ONE SPACE

KINGS ARMS

Goods wagon blocks the road – GO BACK ONE SPACE

Two horses go lame
GO BACK THREE SPACES

Luggage falls from the roof
MISS A TURN

Down hill
MOVE AHEAD ONE SPACE

TRAVELLER'S REST

ARRIVE IN SWANSEA COACHING INN

SWANSEA 3

ARRIVE IN SWANSEA STATION

Boiler bursts
MISS ONE TURN

fresh coal supply
MOVE AHEAD ONE SPACE

Carriage uncouples
GO BACK ONE SPACE

Downhill gradient
MOVE AHEAD TWO SPACES

Bridge over valley
MOVE AHEAD ONE SPACE

Whistle stop to pick up Lord Ashford
MISS A TURN

Name _____

Building a railway

This is a picture showing the route the railway line must take.

♣ Cut out the pictures at the bottom of this page and place them in the spaces where you think they fit best.

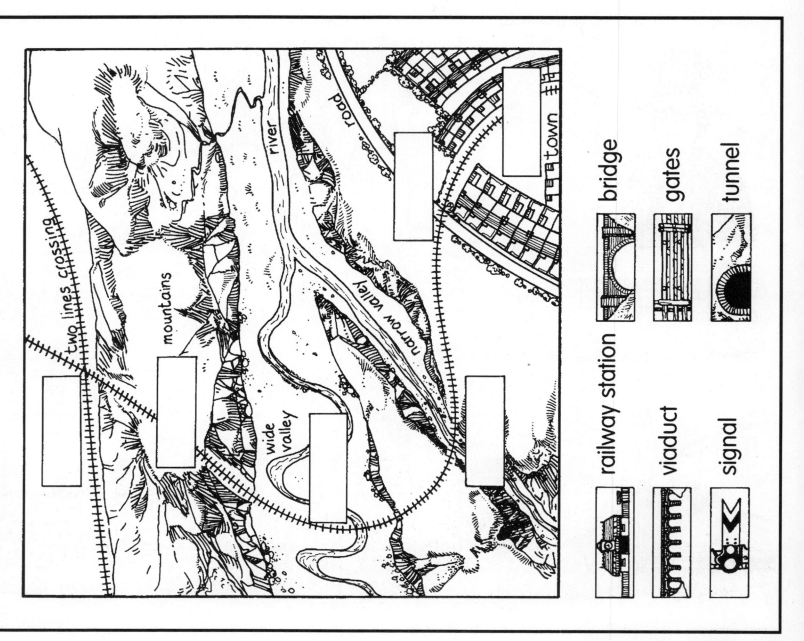

railway station

bridge

viaduct

gates

signal

tunnel

Railway routes: 1

You are the director of the Great Northern Railway Company and your partner is the director of the Great Southern Railway Company.

You are building a railway to the towns marked on the map (the bold squares).

When you reach a town you get the amount of money shown inside that square. You begin with £150 and each square on which you build your railway costs you £10. If you have to build a bridge or dig a tunnel it will cost £20.

T = tunnel
B = bridge

Play this game with a partner.

You will need: a dice, paper and a different coloured pen for each player.

♣ Take turns to roll a dice. The number you throw is the number of squares you may use to build your railway track. If you throw a three you can move three squares.

♣ Draw in your track each turn. Write down your costs and the money you have made at the end of each round.

♣ After ten rounds, count up how much your company has made. The winner is the one with the most profit (money).

Railways

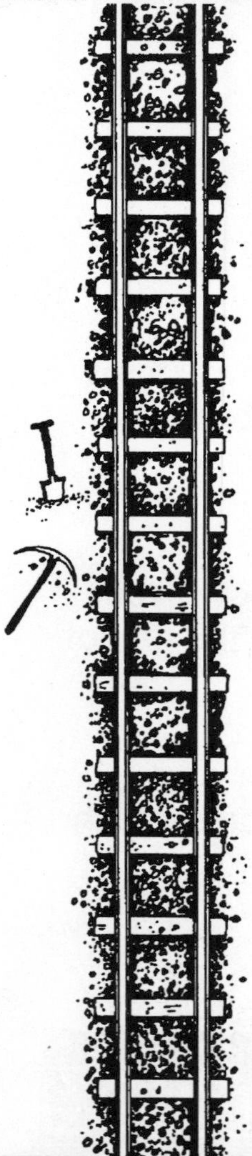

Railway routes: 2

Great Northern
Railway Company
start here

Great Southern
Railway Company
start here

Key

+++++ = Railway line

T = Tunnel

B = Bridge

£ = Towns

Grid contents:
£400, T, £100, B, £100, T
B, B, £50
£200, B
£300, T, B, £300
B, T, T, T
T, £1,000, £200
T
T, T, £200
£300, T, B
£50
£400, B, £400, B
£50

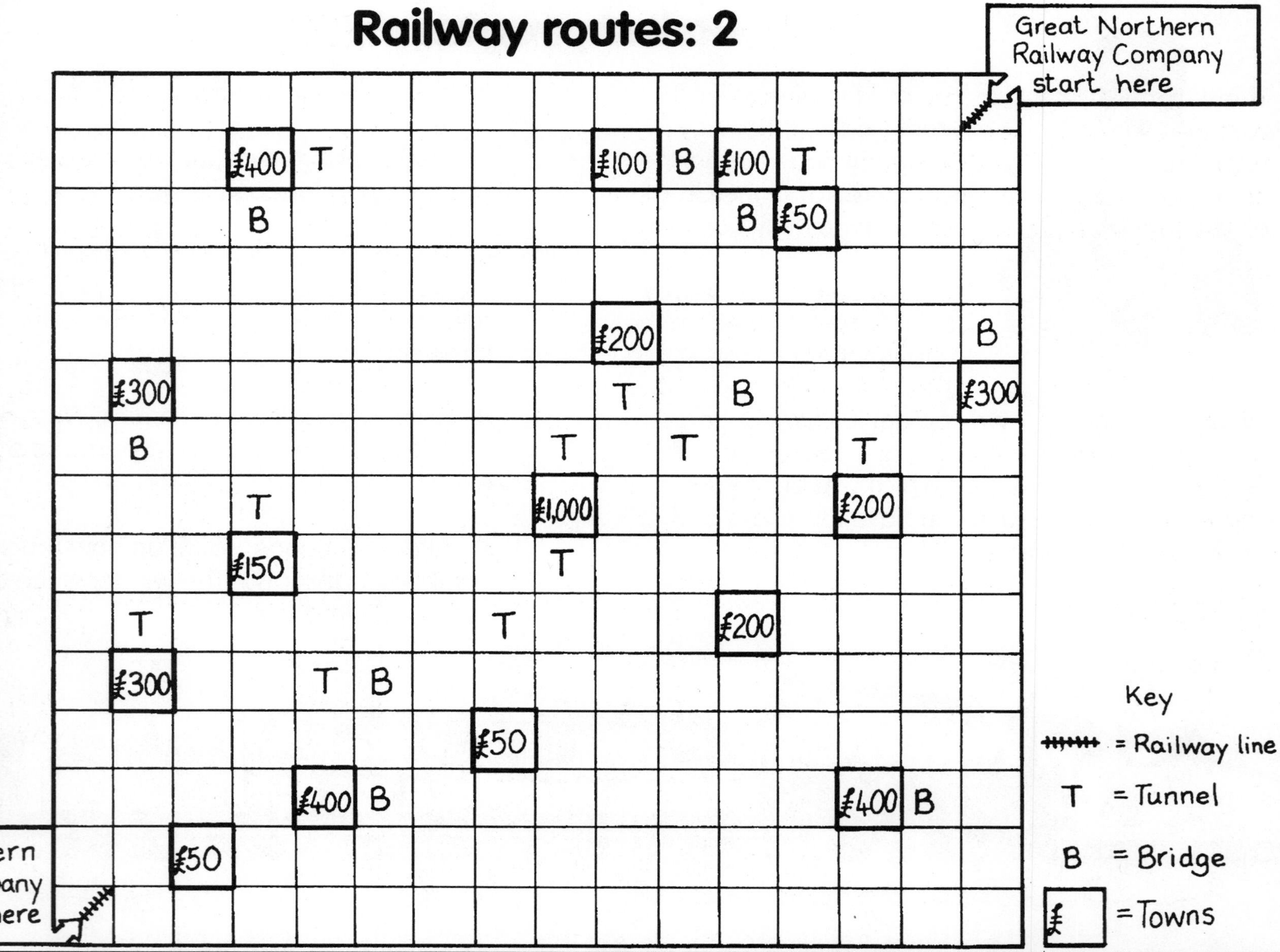

The British Empire, 1897

The Victorians were very proud of their Empire. It was the largest in the history of the world. Children were taught about the wonders of the Empire, and almost every classroom had a map of the world with all the countries of the Empire coloured in red.

✤ Compare this map with a modern atlas of the world. Find the areas shaded below on a modern map. These were all part of the British Empire in 1897. Can you find the names of any of the countries in an atlas? Have any of them changed?

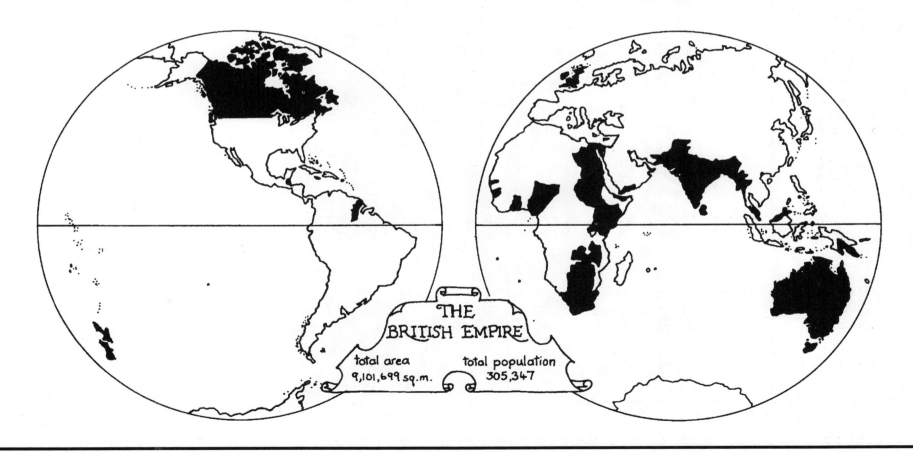

THE BRITISH EMPIRE

total area 9,101,699 sq.m.

total population 305,347

A trading empire

One reason why the British wanted their Empire was for trade. By controlling other lands they could make sure they had a cheap supply of raw materials and native workers. Goods like cotton or rubber were used in factories, while others like tea or coffee were sold in shops. British industries made big profits from these raw materials.

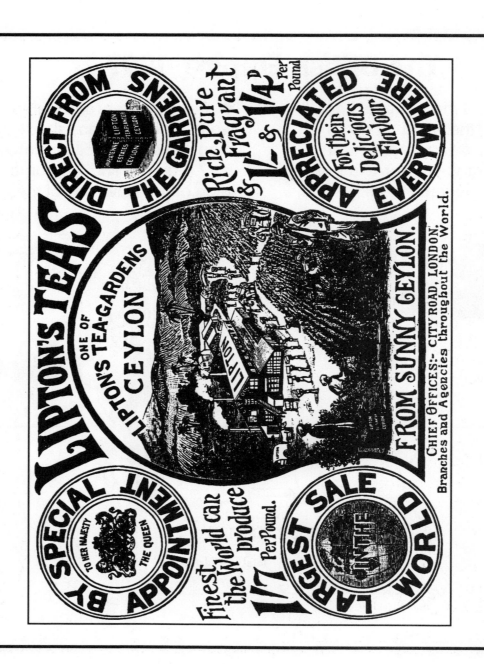

✤ Look at this advertisement from 1887. It shows a tea plantation in Ceylon (now called Sri Lanka).

● What jobs are the native workers doing?
● What animals are used for transport?
● Who is in charge? How can you tell?
● How do we know that Queen Victoria drank Lipton's tea?
● Make a list of all the words used in the advertisement to describe Lipton's tea. Look them up in a thesaurus and choose five other words to describe the taste. On the back of this sheet, make up your own advertisement using these words.

Name _____

A victory for the Empire

The Boer War in South Africa ended in victory for the armies of the Empire in 1902. Celebrations took place all over Britain. The children at Whitburn Church of England School, near Sunderland, were given a special treat. Here is an extract from the school log book.

4 June 1900

School dismissed at 11.35. The children had a holiday in the afternoon to celebrate the capture of Pretoria. Mr and Mrs Haggie gave a treat to all the pupils in the parish, nearly 700. They met at this school at 3.30 and each child was given a small brooch in the shape of the Union Jack. The teachers were given a medal with a three coloured ribbon.

All of the children marched round the village and opposite the Haggies' house sang 'God Save the Queen'. At 4.30 a splendid tea was given in the recreation ground. Games followed until 7.30 when the Reverend Ashwell thanked the Haggies for their kindness. The Headmaster then said that Mr and Mrs Haggie would be well rewarded if the boys and girls grew up to be loyal subjects of our noble Queen. On leaving, each child was presented with a photo of Lord Roberts (the top British soldier in South Africa).

✤ Find three different ways in which this treat was meant to make the children proud of their country.

✤ We are not told what was on the medal given to the teachers. If you were Mr and Mrs Haggie, what words and pictures would you have told the maker to put on it? Design each side of your medal in the space below.

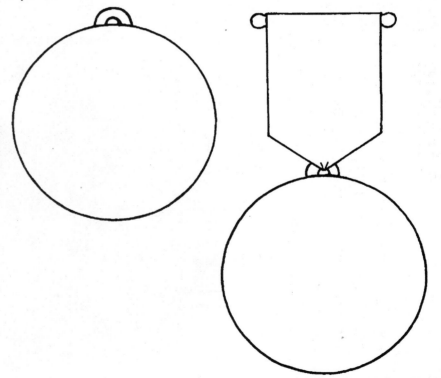

Name _____

Leaving the Highlands: 1

The government wanted to make the Empire strong by encouraging British people to emigrate, that is to go to live in the colonies. Many Scots chose to do this, hoping to make a better life for themselves in Canada or Australia, where land was cheap. Others were given no choice. In the 1840s, thousands of highlanders were driven off their lands by landlords who wanted to turn their farms into grazing land for sheep.

Teacher Timesavers: Victorian Britain

Leaving the Highlands: 2

✤ Look carefully at the drawing on Leaving the Highlands: 1. It is based on a Victorian picture showing a highlander and his wife sailing away from their home.

✤ In the bubbles on this page with solid edges write what you think the people are saying to each other.

✤ In the bubbles with dotted edges write what you think they are thinking.

✤ Now cut the bubbles and the picture out and stick them on to paper, matching the speech and thought bubbles with the right people.

Name _____

Pity the poor emigrant

Sean Murdoch leaned over the top bunk and was violently sick as the emigrant ship Wandsworth *was thrown about in a storm-tossed sea. This voyage was sheer misery.*

Ten-year-old Sean and his family had left Ireland to escape a land ruined by famine. A terrible disease had turned the potato crops into mush in the ground. This brought death from starvation to many poor peasants who relied on one crop. The young went first. The thin and wasted bodies of Sean's two brothers had been buried wrapped in a cloth. They had no money for coffins.

The Murdochs' only chance was a new life in Canada, helped with money from the parish priest. They sailed from Dublin in June 1847, bound for what the advertisements called 'the flourishing city of Quebec'. But their ship became a prison. The sailors stole their few possessions, the drinking water was bitter and their food had to be paid for. Soon ship fever broke out and people lay moaning on their bunks until the breath left them.

Sean's father had fought the fever for two days before his big-framed body was left thin and hollow. The sailors had dragged him from the steerage hold where the emigrants lay packed together and tipped his corpse into the sea without a Christian prayer. His mother, too weak to help her husband, was also ill with typhus. Soon they would land at Grosse Island, 30 miles down the St Lawrence river from Quebec City. This was the quarantine station where all those who were ill would be kept in fever hospitals, almost certain to die.

✤ Read the passage. Why did Sean's family want to go to Canada?

✤ Look up typhus in a dictionary. What causes it? Why would it spread quickly on a crowded ship?

✤ Why do you think the sailors treated the emigrants so badly? On the back of this sheet, write a page from the diary of a sailor in which he explains his feelings about the passengers.

✤ What should Sean do? If he stays with his mother they might both die on Grosse Island. Will they escape? Will his mother recover? Will they begin a new life? Finish off the story.

Name _____

An arrogant empire

Robinson Crusoe was written by Daniel Defoe in the eighteenth century but was very popular with the Victorians. In the story, a brave and intelligent white man becomes master of the island on which his ship is wrecked. He saves a black man who becomes his faithful servant and whom he names Friday.

This was the way many people liked to think of the British Empire in the world – taming wild lands and people to make them useful. The British came to believe that they were better than any other country or people.

✣ This picture of Robinson Crusoe and Man Friday is taken from a book printed during Victorian times. What is happening? Do you think white Victorians saw anything wrong with this picture?

✣ Very few black people lived in Victorian Britain. How do you think this affected what ordinary British people felt about them?

Name _____

Words from the Empire

The British picked up thousands of words from the peoples they conquered and added them to the English language, making it more varied and colourful. Look at the list of words. How many have you heard before? All of them came from countries that were part of the Empire.

✤ Look up these words in a dictionary and write out their meanings.

✤ See if you can find out which languages the words came from and if their meaning has changed since first being used in English.

✤ Write a story which uses as many of these words as possible. Begin: *John left the bungalow and rushed down the street in his khaki dungarees...*

bungalow   calico catamaran

chintz   chutney   curry   dinghy

dungarees gingham   gymkhana

juggernaut   jungle   khaki

pyjamas   shampoo   shawl

teak   veranda   yoga

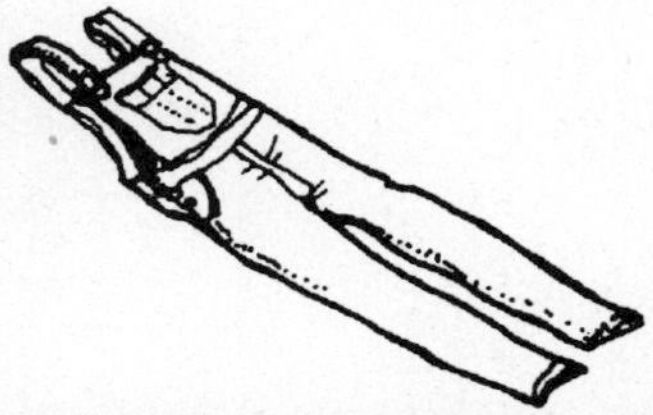

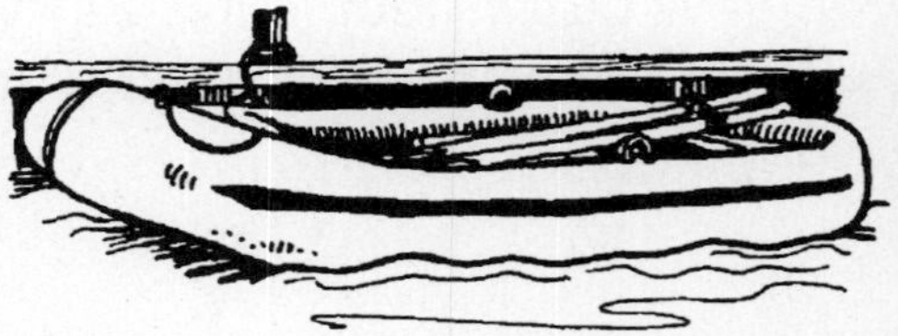

Queen Victoria's Diamond Jubilee Parade (1897): 1

In 1897, the British celebrated 60 years of Queen Victoria's reign. A military parade through the streets of London included troops from all over the Empire and was a display of Britain's strength across the world.

♣ Colour in the soldiers' uniforms. Look at the key on sheet 2 to help with this, and use your imagination for any parts you are not sure about.

♣ Compare the Victorian uniforms with those of modern-day soldiers. What do you notice? Why do you think Victorian soldiers wore such bright colours?

♣ Cut out the soldiers and use them to make a frieze or wall display of Queen Victoria's Jubilee Parade.

Gold Coast Haussas

Bikanir Camel Corps

Borneo Dyaks

Queen Victoria's Diamond Jubilee Parade (1897): 2

South Australian
Mounted Rifles

Cape Mounted
Rifles

Gold Coast Haussas – blue uniforms with red jacket edges and white boots.
South Australian Mounted Rifles – light khaki uniforms and black boots.
Borneo Dyaks – light khaki uniforms and black boots, native dress (as colourful as you like).
Cape Mounted Rifles – dark khaki uniforms, white hats.
Bikanir Camel Corps – green jacket and white trousers.

Name _____

Before and after

Below are some pictures showing important Victorian inventions.

✤ Alongside each invention draw:

a) what you imagine existed or was used before this item was invented;
b) a modern version of this invention.

After		
Victorian	camera · telephone · gramophone · electric light · sewing machine	
Before		

Communication

Messages in Morse Code

In 1840, the American Samuel Morse invented Morse Code, an alphabet made from dots and dashes. A dot was a short signal and a dash a long signal. The message could be written or sent using light or sound signals.

Below you can see the Morse Code alphabet.

✤ Write out your name in Morse Code. Can others read it?

✤ Now make up your own short emergency message and flash it by torch across the room to a friend. Can they read it? Remember: dot = short flash, dash = long flash.

A	B	C	D	E	F	G	H	I
·—	—···	—·—·	—··	·	··—·	——·	····	··

J	K	L	M	N	O	P	Q	R
·———	—·—	·—··	——	—·	———	·——·	——·—	·—·

S	T	U	V	W	X	Y	Z	FULL STOP
···	—	··—	···—	·——	—··—	—·——	——··	·—·—·—

Name _____

Electrical experiments

During Victorian times, many scientists and inventors began experimenting with electricity. Try out these experiments with electricity to see what you can discover.

You will need: a battery; three bulbs and bulb holders; insulated wire with bare ends. (NB Make sure the voltage of the battery and the bulbs is the same.)

✤ Use the battery, wires, a bulb and a bulb holder to make a circuit.

✤ Add another bulb to the circuit. What happens to the brightness of the bulbs?

✤ What happens if you add a third bulb to the circuit?

✤ Remove one of the bulbs from its holder. What happens?

✤ Find a way to connect a battery and two bulbs so that if one bulb is removed the other stays on.

✤ Make a circuit using a battery, wires, a bulb and a bulb holder. At one point make a break in the circuit.

✤ Now use a selection of materials to fill the break in the circuit. (You could use: a paper-clip; a rubber; a pencil; a plastic spoon; a metal spoon; a drawing pin or other materials if you wish.)

✤ What happens to the bulb each time? Is there a pattern to the type of material that will let the electricity flow and allow the bulb to light?

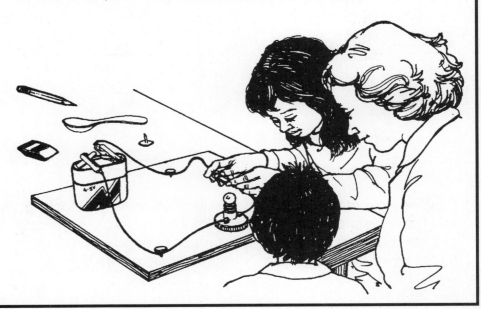

Lighting

Lighting a house

In Victorian times the sort of lighting you had in your house depended on when you were born and how wealthy you were. Most people relied on one of the following for light.

✤ Do you have any of these kinds of light in your house? Have you ever used any of the other kinds of lamp? What are the advantages and disadvantages of each kind of light?

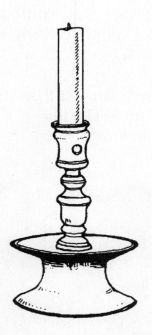

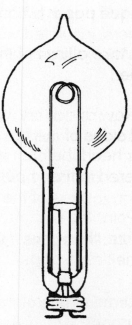

Candles were made from the fat of animals such as whales and seals. The wick soaks up the fat which burns at the tip.

Oil lamps burned vegetable or animal oils. In the 1860s people started to use paraffin oil which burned much more brightly.

Gas was made from coal and brought into houses by pipe. At first the gas flame was bare, but in 1893 cheap mantles made the flame burn more brightly.

Electric lamps became available in the 1880s after Joseph Swan had invented the light bulb. It gave a bright, safe light but was very expensive.

Make a pinhole camera

✤ Take a cardboard box and cut a large rectangular hole in two facing sides.

✤ Cover one hole with transparent tissue or greaseproof paper, then cover the other with opaque paper (which you cannot see through).

✤ Make a tiny hole in the centre of the opaque paper.

✤ Now attach a large piece of dark cloth to the top and sides of the box so that if you use this to cover your head, before looking at the side of the box covered in tissue paper, no light can get in.

✤ Point the pinhole at a window or other light source, then cover your head with the cloth and look at the tissue paper.

✤ Draw what you see. What do you notice about the image?

✤ Make other pinholes in the opaque paper. What happens to the image?

✤ Make a slightly larger hole in the paper. What happens now?

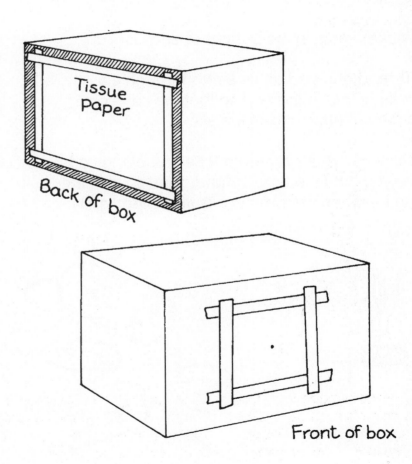

Telephones

Name _____

Make a string telephone

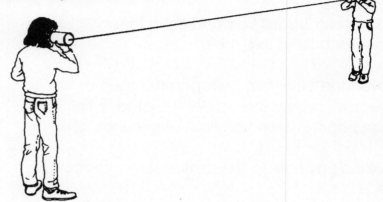

You will need: two empty tin cans; paper cups or yoghurt cartons and a piece of string several metres in length.

✤ Make a hole in the bottom of each tin can.

✤ Thread one end of the string through each hole then tie a knot in the end so that the cans are attached to each end of the string.

✤ Now ask your partner to take one of the cans while you hold the other. Stand apart so that the string between the two cans is stretched tightly.

✤ Take it in turn to speak into your tin while the other person listens. Can you hear what is being said?

✤ Can you say why this works?

✤ What happens if you alter the length of the piece of string? Can you hear more clearly?

✤ What happens if you use wire or fishing line instead of string?

✤ Try using containers made from different materials instead of tin cans. Does this make a difference?

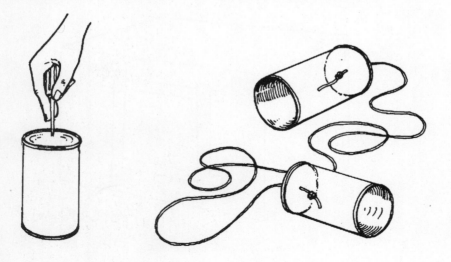

Moving pictures: 1

Before cinema and television the Victorians invented a machine called the 'zoetrope' which created the illusion of moving images. Try this activity to make your own zoetrope.

✤ Colour in the drawings on Moving pictures: 2, then cut out the two picture strips.

✤ Cut a piece of card 50cm x 20cm, then stick the picture strips end to end along the baseline of this piece of card.

✤ Allow a gap of 2cm above the picture strip, then cut vertical slots above each figure (8cm x 0.5cm).

✤ Now bend the strip round to make a circle and stick the ends together using sticky tape. Make sure that the pictures are on the inside of the circle.

✤ Draw a circle on stiff card to fit the base of this circle and pierce a small hole through its centre.

✤ Cut out the circle on card and attach it to the base of your picture strip circle.

✤ Make a cardboard cone, then stick a pin through the hole in the centre of the base of the zoetrope and down into the top of the cone.

✤ Now spin the zoetrope and look through the slots at the pictures as it spins. What can you see?

A zoetrope

Moving pictures: 2

Milestones in medicine: 1

Many important discoveries in the field of medicine were made during the Victorian period.

✤ Cut out these 'milestones' and arrange them in the order in which they happened to make a timeline.

✤ Why would Lister and Koch have been unable to do their work without the discoveries of Pasteur?

✤ Look up 'pasteurisation' in a dictionary. What does it mean? What happens when milk reaches a temperature of 140°F (60° C)?

Florence Nightingale set up a hospital for wounded soldiers in 1854 during the Crimean War. When she returned to Britain she set up the Nightingale School for nurses.

In Germany, Robert Koch began work to find out which germs caused which diseases. In 1882, he identified the germ that caused tuberculosis, a disease that resulted in many deaths.

Medicine

Milestones in medicine: 2

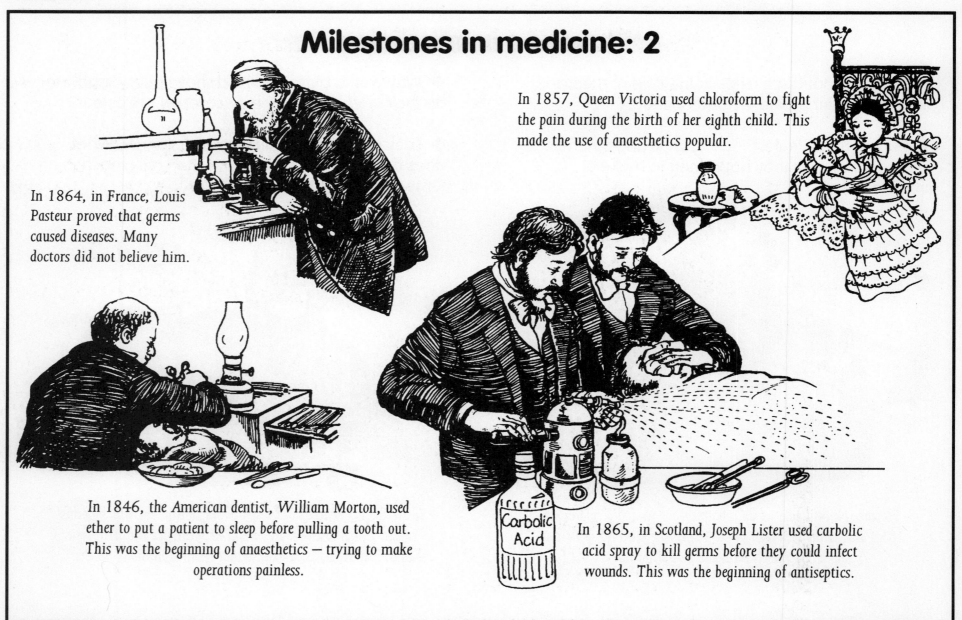

In 1864, in France, Louis Pasteur proved that germs caused diseases. Many doctors did not believe him.

In 1857, Queen Victoria used chloroform to fight the pain during the birth of her eighth child. This made the use of anaesthetics popular.

In 1846, the American dentist, William Morton, used ether to put a patient to sleep before pulling a tooth out. This was the beginning of anaesthetics — trying to make operations painless.

Carbolic Acid

In 1865, in Scotland, Joseph Lister used carbolic acid spray to kill germs before they could infect wounds. This was the beginning of antiseptics.

The *Great Britain*

Isambard Kingdom Brunel was one of the greatest Victorian engineers. He built railways, bridges and steamships. His most famous ship was the SS *Great Britain*.

♣ Look carefully at the picture and read the passage below. Describe the main features of the *Great Britain*. Label parts of the ship wherever you can.

♣ If the *Great Britain* had engines, why do you think Brunel included masts and sails?

♣ Use chalk to mark out on the playground the size of the propeller.

Isambard Kingdom Brunel

I am very proud of this ship. When she was launched in Bristol in 1843 the Great Britain was the most up-to-date design in the world. She was 322ft long and 50.5ft wide. The hull was made of iron and she had a huge propeller, 15ft in diameter with six blades. The 1,000 horsepower steam engines drove her at a speed of up to 11 knots on her first voyage – across the Atlantic from Liverpool to New York. None of these ideas was completely new but no-one before me had put them together before in such a big ship, 3,500 tons.

Power and propulsion

Name _____

Sail or steam?

The diagrams on this page give some ideas for powering a model boat. Try them out. Can you think of any other ways to power a model boat? Try these out too.

♣ Which was the fastest? Record your results in the table below, in order from the fastest to the slowest. Which type of power do you think is the best? Give your reasons.

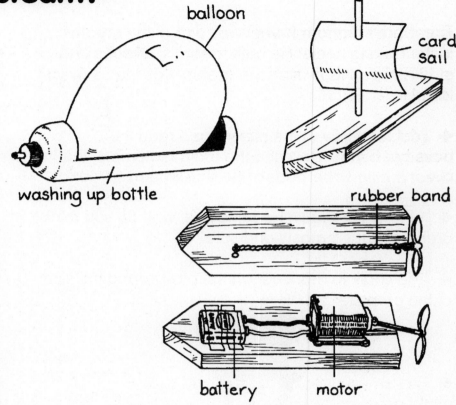

balloon

card sail

washing up bottle

rubber band

battery   motor

type of power in order of speed

♣ How would powered ships have been an improvement on sailing ships?

♣ Why do you think it would have been important to have fast ships for carrying certain types of cargo (goods)?

Name _____

These advertisements were printed in the *National Telephone Directory* in 1897. They show some of the latest inventions of the day.

❧ Which one do you think would have been most useful? Tick that box.

☐ **a bicycle**

☐ **a typewriter**

☐ **electric lighting**

☐ **a telephone**

❧ Explain your choice and how it might have made life easier.

All mod cons!

L. M. ERICSSON & Co.,
STOCKHOLM.

TELEGRAPHIC ADDRESS MERCFON, STOCKHOLM

Manufacturing and Export Worldwide

TELEPHONE, TELEGRAPH and

FIRE-ALARM APPARATUS

CENTRAL and MULTIPLE SWITCHBOARD

For Single and Double Circuits

TESTING INSTRUMENTS

Yearly output 35,000 complete Sets of Telephone Instruments

FIRST CLASS WORKMANSHIP and DURABILITY

CATALOGUES FREE OF CHARGE

THE ENGLISH CLEVELAND

TELEGRAMS 'SAFES', WOLVERHAMPTON

THE CYCLE FOR '97

Made by the OLDEST FIRM of CYCLE MANUFACTURERS

GEORGE PRICE, ld

CYCLE ENGINEERS

WOLVERHAMPTON

WRITE FOR NEW PRICE LISTS
SOLE AGENTS WANTED

THE WORLD RENOWNED
"EDISWAN" LAMPS
OF ALL VOLTAGES.

☞ THE BEST and the CHEAPEST in the end

THE EDISON & SWAN UNITED ELECTRIC LIGHT COMPANY LIMITED

MANUFACTURERS AND CONTRACTORS TO the BRITISH ADMIRALTY, POST OFFICE, WAR OFFICE, BRITISH RAILWAYS, ELECTRIC LIGHT COMPANIES, NATIONAL TELEPHONE COMPANY, COLONIAL GOVERNMENTS

SEE ALL LAMPS ARE MARKED EDISWAN

THE "LIGHT RUNNING" "BALL BEARING"
DENSMORE TYPEWRITER

DO YOU WANT TO SAVE TIME, WORRY AND EXPENSE?
DO YOU WANT an uptodate Typewriter that challenges the world to produce its equal in modern conveniences?
THE NEW NO 2 DENSMORE STANDS TODAY BEST THE WORLD OVER.

A special description circular in return for your name

United Typewriter & Supplies Co.,
85 & 86 QUEEN ST., LONDON, E.C.

BIRMINGHAM	MANCHESTER
GLASGOW	EDINBURGH
LIVERPOOL	BELFAST

Hymns

Name _____

All things bright and beautiful

This is a verse and the chorus of a famous hymn written during Victorian times.

❖ Read the verse. What does it tell us about rich and poor people in the Victorian period?

❖ What does the hymn tell us about their religious beliefs?

❖ Make up another verse about their religious beliefs. Write it in the space below.

❖ Can you find the hymn in a hymn book? What do the other verses say?

All things bright and beautiful
All creatures great and small
All things wise and wonderful
The Lord God made them all. (chorus)

The rich man in his castle
The poor man at his gate
God made them high and lowly
And ordered their estate*. (verse)

*ordered their estate = God made rich and poor classes of people.

Religious ABC

The Victorians used the Christian Bible stories in many different ways. Here is an example from a schoolbook.

♣ Read the Christian ABC. Now take the letters E, F, G and make up a rhyme based on the stories in The Bible.

 is an *Angel* who praises the Lord

 is for *Bible, God's* most holy word

 is for church where the religious resort*

 is for devil who wishes our hurt

*resort = to go

 _____

_____

 _____

_____

 _____

_____

Name _____

Religious numbers

The following activity from a Victorian schoolbook
uses the Bible as a starting point for maths work.
Can you do these sums?

12 *disciples added to the* **4** *gospels makes*

7 *loaves added to* **5** *fishes makes*

Jesus had **12** *disciples.* **1** *of the disciples, Judas Iscariot,
hanged himself. How many disciples were left?*

God made the world in **7** *days but rested on the last*
1 *(day). How many days did it take to make the world?*

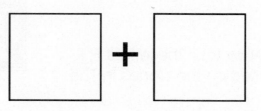

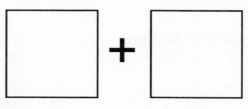

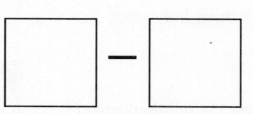

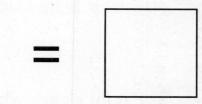

Name _____

Victorian Christmas: 1

Queen Victoria's husband, Prince Albert, brought the idea of decorating a Christmas tree to England from his home in Germany.

✤ Photocopy the tree outline twice on to stiff card. Cut out the tree shapes and cut slits into the branches where indicated. Make the Christmas tree as shown below.

✤ Now look at Victorian Christmas: 2.

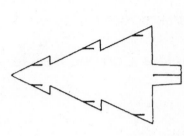

Tree A: cut a slot from the top down to where the branches end.

Tree B: cut a slot from the bottom of the tree up to where the branches begin.

Now slot Tree B into Tree A and fix the base with Plasticine.

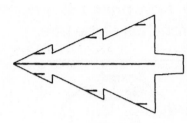

Name _____

Victorian Christmas: 2

✤ Look at the presents on this page.

✤ Now look at the labels below. Can you decide who each present is for?

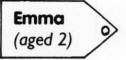
Emma
(aged 2)

Victoria
(aged 9)

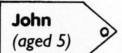
John
(aged 5)

George
(aged 10)

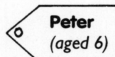
Peter
(aged 6)

✤ Now cut the labels and presents out and make a small hole through the circle on each.

✤ Match each present with the correct label.

✤ Thread a short length of cotton through the holes of the label and present card for each pair and tie the ends together to make a small loop.

✤ Now hang the presents in the slots on the branches of the tree.

Christmas cards

Sending Christmas cards began during Queen Victoria's reign. A man called Henry Cole was probably the first man who thought of sending Christmas cards. This is the card he designed.

♣ Draw your own Christmas card to send in the space on the right. It must show a Christmas scene from Victorian times.

♣ Complete the verse to go inside your Christmas card in the space below.

Be of good cheer for this is the time

Of feasting and laughing and drinking mulled wine

_____

_____

Christian duty

Here is a list of some of the charities in the busy port and ship-building town of Sunderland in 1890.

✤ Which of these charities show that Sunderland was a port? What problems were they trying to help?

✤ Imagine that you are a wealthy ship-builder and want to set up a charity to help the families of men injured working in the shipyards. What kind of help would you offer and how would you organise this?

✤ At your local studies library or archives, look in the Victorian street directories for your area. Can you find a list of local charities? What sort of people did they look after?

The Donnison School – *every year 36 poor girls were educated and given clothes.*

The Sunderland Orphan Asylum – *provided a home for 40 boys and tried to find them jobs at sea when they left.*

The Pottery Buildings – *gave free teas and medical advice to foreign seamen and other workmen. It was run by a manager who could speak several languages.*

The Blind Institute – *employed 40 blind men and women. There was a library of 3,000 Morse books (books with raised Morse Code dots that could be read with a finger, like Braille).*

The Seamen's Mission – *provided a reading room, refreshments and entertainment for foreign seamen.*

The Provident Dispensary – *if a family paid 1s a month they were given any medical treatment they needed.*

Trafalgar Square Aged Seamen's Asylum – *offered homes to old sailors and sailors' widows.*

The demon drink

Many poor Victorians turned to drinking alcohol in an attempt to forget the troubles of their hard lives. But this brought problems of its own, and organisations were founded to persuade people not to drink alcohol.

♣ Look at the picture on this page. What do you think the little girl is saying?

_____

_____

_____

_____

_____

_____

♣ The picture is based on a Victorian drawing with the title 'Between drink and duty'. Explain in your own words what this means. Can you think of a better title?

Name _____

Graveyard studies

Victorians often set up ornate gravestones in memory of their family or friends. These inscriptions come from the graveyard of St Mary's Church, Whitby.

SACRED to the memory of Thomas Burnett, Master Mariner, who perished with the whole of his crew on their passage from St Andrews on or about the 7th January 1834, aged 39 years. ELIZABETH, his daughter, died February 22 1830, aged 9 months. WILLIAM, his son, died October 29th 1843, aged 12 years.

HERE LIE THE REMAINS OF EDWARD PENNOCK MASTER MARINER WHO DEPARTED THIS LIFE MAY 22, 1847, AGED 56 YEARS
Though Boreas' blast and Neptune's waves have tossed me to and fro
Yet it is by God's decree I harbour here below
Where I at anchor ride with many of our fleet
Hoping one day to rise again our Saviour Christ to meet

SACRED to the memory of JOHN HENRY, son of GEORGE and ELIZABETH VASEY, who died August 24 1836, aged 2 years. Also Thomas their son who died in his infancy. Also the above ELIZABETH VASEY who died March 16th 1856.
Early bright transient as morning dew
They sparkled were exhaled and went to heaven

Sacred to the memory of JOHN BARRITT, pilot, who was drowned off Whitby, December 29th 1845, aged 57 years.

Tomorrow I will better live
Is not for men to say
Tomorrow can no surety give
The wise make sure today.

Also HANNAH, his wife, who died June 18th 1853, aged 62 years.

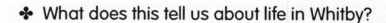

❧ What does this tell us about life in Whitby?

❧ Why do you think Thomas Burnett's family are not sure exactly when he died?

❧ What do the poems tell us about what the Victorians believed about death?

Teacher Timesavers: Victorian Britain

Name _____

Graveyard inscriptions

♣ Use this sheet to collect inscriptions from your local graveyard. Remember to write the words in the same place and to spell them exactly as they are on the headstone.

Teacher Timesavers: Victorian Britain

125

Memorial stones

Depending on their taste and how much money they had, Victorians could choose from many memorials to mark the graves of their relatives. Here are some common Victorian memorial stones.

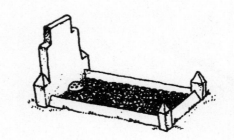

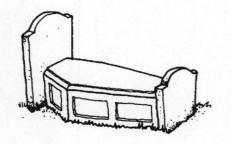

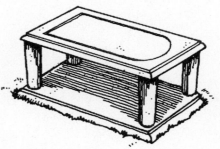

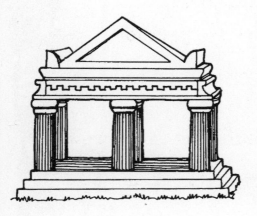

❖ Can you find any memorials similar to these in your local churchyard or cemetery?

❖ What other designs can you find? Photograph or draw them to make a display.

❖ Design your own memorial for a family grave.

A Victorian holiday

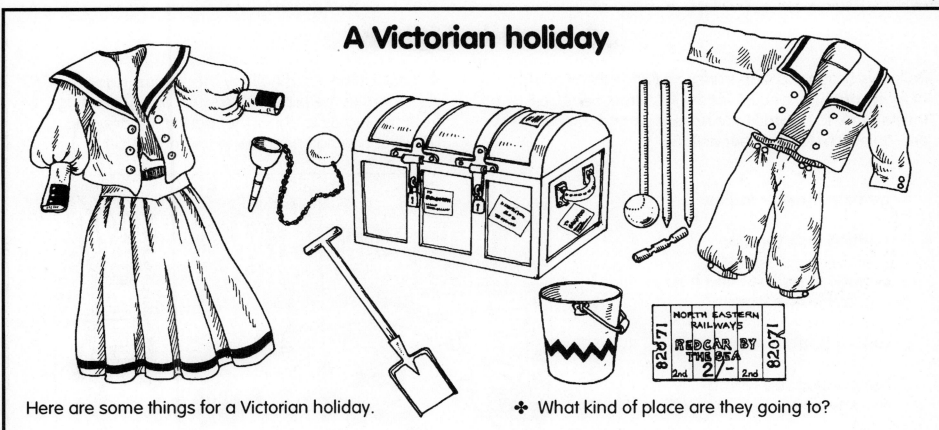

Here are some things for a Victorian holiday.

❖ Look carefully at the pictures.

❖ How many people do you think are going on holiday?

❖ How are they getting to the place where they will spend their holiday?

❖ What kind of place are they going to?

❖ What do you think they will do when they go on holiday?

❖ How do you know the answers to these questions?

❖ What other questions would you want to ask about their holidays?

Name _____

A seaside holiday

Railways brought cheap transport within the reach of many ordinary people for the first time. Seaside towns grew to provide lodging, shops and entertainment for the new visitors.

❖ Look at the list of holiday attractions. Can you spot them in the picture? Draw an arrow pointing from the words to show that part of the drawing. (The first one has been done for you.)

bathing huts for ladies

bathing huts for men

a horse to pull bathing huts in and out of the water

rowing boats for hire

the promenade with a road behind

boarding houses and hotels

children playing in the sea

women holding umbrellas to protect themselves from the sun

Name _____

Wish you were here

♣ Imagine you are on holiday in the summer of 1890 and are sending a postcard to a friend.

♣ Colour in the postcard scene below.

♣ Fill in the name and address of the person you are sending the card to, then write your message. You might want to tell them about the weather, your journey, what you have done on the beach and so on.

♣ Now cut out both sides of your postcard and stick them to a piece of card to make your own postcard.

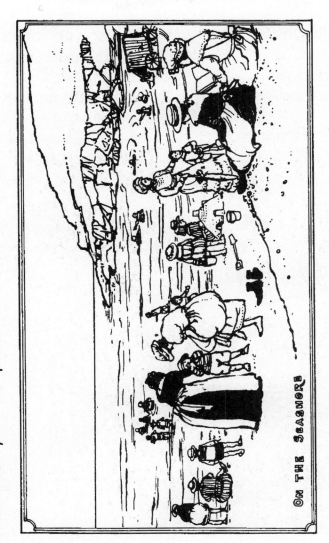

ON THE SEASHORE

POST CARD

THIS SPACE FOR INLAND, COLONIAL AND CERTAIN FOREIGN CORRESPONDENCE.

THE ADDRESS ONLY TO BE WRITTEN HERE

NATIONAL SERIES

INLAND POSTAGE ½d
FOREIGN POSTAGE 1d

MILLAR & LANG Ltd.,
(PRINTED IN BRITAIN)

Name _____

Victorian parks

Many fine parks were set up by the Victorians.

✤ Take this checklist with you to your local park. Tick the boxes next to those that you can see.

✤ What is the name of your local park? Is it named after a famous person, family or event?

✤ Can you find any more Victorian features, or others added at a later date?

✤ Sketch or photograph the features in your park, especially if they look different from the ones on this sheet. With your friends, make a display of the things you saw.

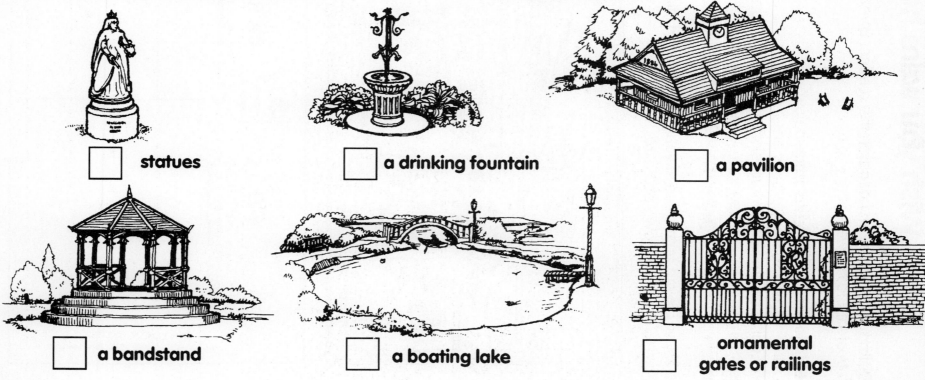

☐ **statues**

☐ **a drinking fountain**

☐ **a pavilion**

☐ **a bandstand**

☐ **a boating lake**

☐ **ornamental gates or railings**

For sale

Dolls' houses were very popular with children. Some of them had lots of detail and were very expensive to buy.

♣ Imagine that this dolls' house is for sale. Write a description of the house and, on the back of this sheet, draw a picture to show the buyers what it looks like from the outside.

Name _____

Making Victorian figures

The diagram on the right shows how you can make a model figure.

❖ Now make other figures to represent a rich Victorian family and a poor Victorian family. Use coloured paper or card or pieces of material to make clothes for your figures. (Use reference books if you are not sure how people used to dress.)

❖ Imagine that the poor family work for the rich family. What jobs do they all do?

❖ Some silver spoons go missing from the rich household. Make up a story about what has happened. Are the spoons found? Who is blamed and what happens to them?

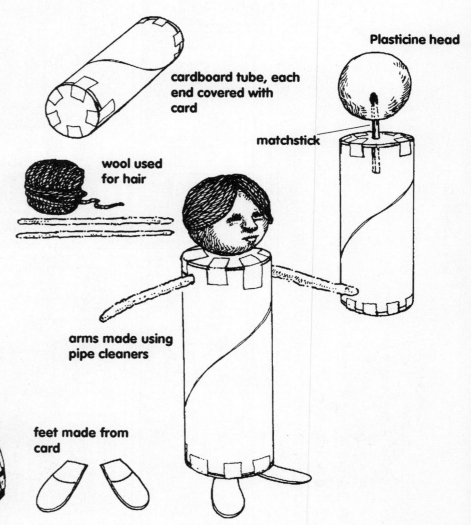

cardboard tube, each end covered with card

Plasticine head

matchstick

wool used for hair

arms made using pipe cleaners

feet made from card

Teacher Timesavers: Victorian Britain

What sport are they playing?

Many of the sports we play today were invented or became popular during Victorian times.

♣ Can you name each of the sports below? Write the name of the sport below each picture.

Name _____

Women and sport

Advertisements can tell us a lot about how people used to live.

♣ What sports are the women in these advertisements playing?

♣ What is being advertised? Look up 'embrocation' in a dictionary to help you.

♣ What is the 'catchphrase' for these advertisements? What does it mean?

♣ Look carefully at how the women are drawn.
• How do the pictures show that women are becoming more equal to men?
• How do they show that women still had limits placed on what they could do?

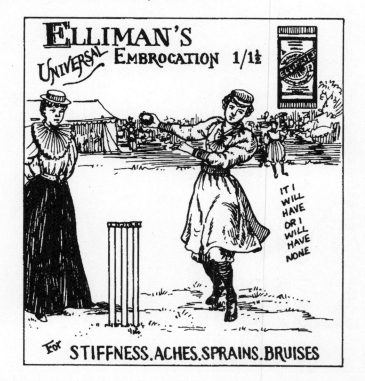

Name _____

A street game

Most Victorian children had little money and made up games to play in the street. This game was called 'bays' in the north of England.

♣ In order to play, chalk out the pattern on this page on the playground. Each bay must be big enough to stand in. Find a small, flat stone. This was called a 'dabber'.

♣ Slide the dabber along the ground into bay 1. Hop into bay 1, pick up the stone and hop back to the start line.

♣ Slide the dabber into bay 2. Hop into bay 1, then bay 2 and pick up the stone. Hop back to the start.

♣ Slide the dabber into bay 3. Jump so that when you land one foot is in bay 1 and the other in bay 2. Hop into bay 3, pick up the dabber then hop round, jump so that your feet land in bays 1 and 2 and return to the start.

♣ Carry on like this. Hop into single bays and jump so that both feet land in bays that are side by side.

So: bays 1 and 2 (jump), bay 3 (hop), bays 4 and 5 (jump), bay 6 (hop) and so on ...

REMEMBER

If you miss the bay you are aiming for with the dabber you lose that turn.

If your foot touches a line, you miss a turn.

If you lose your balance when picking up the dabber or make a mistake and hop or jump into the wrong bay you lose that turn.

Return to the start after each turn.

Paintings

Name _____

Victorian paintings

Victorian popular paintings often showed sad events and were meant to move those who looked at them.

❖ Look at this picture. Together with the children on your table, decide:
- what has just happened;
- what the people are thinking;
- what you think is about to happen.

❖ With the other children in your group, act out what is happening in the picture. Try to stand exactly like the people in the picture and see if other children in the class can guess what is happening.

❖ In the same way, try to show what happened before and immediately after the scene in the picture.

Victorian writers

There were many Victorian writers whose books are still read today.

❖ Match the titles of the books with the people who wrote them.

❖ Find out what the stories are about and draw a cover for one of the books.

Lewis Carroll

Charles Dickens

Robert Louis Stevenson

Charles Kingsley

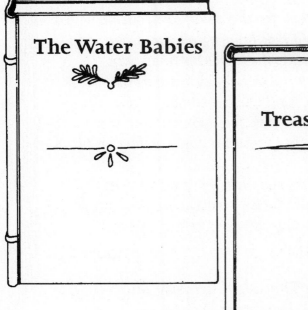
The Water Babies

Treasure Island

Oliver Twist

Alice in Wonderland

Name _____

Victorian books: 1

This is an extract from a book by Charles Dickens, a famous writer from Victorian times.

❧ Read through the passage on this page.

❧ Draw a picture to show what is happening.

❧ Write down what you think has happened before this part of the story and what happens next.

It was a dirty little box, this counting house, with nothing in it but an old rickety desk and two stools, a hat-peg, an ancient almanac, an inkstand with no ink, and the stump of one pen, and an eight-day clock which hadn't gone for eighteen years at least, and of which the minute-hand had been twisted off for a tooth-pick. Daniel Quilp pulled his hat over his brows, climbed on to the desk (which had a flat top), and, stretching his short length upon it, went to sleep.

He had not been asleep a quarter of an hour when the boy opened the door and thrust in his head. Quilp was a light sleeper and started up directly.

'Here's somebody for you,' said the boy.

'Who?'

'I don't know.'

'Ask, you dog,' said Quilp, seizing his piece of wood and preparing to throw it at the boy.

At that moment the visitor presented herself at the door.

'What, Nelly!' cried Quilp.

'Yes,' said the child, hesitating whether to enter or retreat, for the dwarf just roused, with his dishevelled hair hanging all about him, and a yellow handkerchief over his head, was something fearful to behold; 'it's only me, sir.'

'Come in,' said Quilp, without getting off the desk. 'Come in. Stay. Just look out into the yard and see whether there's a boy standing on his head.'

'No, sir,' replied Nell. 'He's on his feet.'

'You're sure he is?' said Quilp. 'Well. Now come in and shut the door. What's your message, Nelly?'

From The Old Curiosity Shop
by Charles Dickens

Victorian books: 2

This is an extract from a book by Lewis Carroll, a famous writer from Victorian times.

✤ Read through the passage on this page.

✤ Draw a picture to show what is happening in the story in the space below.

✤ Write down what you think has happened before this part of the story and what you think happens next.

The rabbit-hole went straight on like a tunnel for some way, and then dipped suddenly down, so suddenly that Alice had not a moment to think about stopping herself before she found herself falling down what seemed to be a very deep well.

Either the well was very deep, or she fell very slowly, for she had plenty of time as she went down to look about her, and to wonder what was going to happen next. First, she tried to look down and make out what she was coming to, but it was too dark to see anything; then she looked at the sides of the well and noticed that they were filled with cupboards and book-shelves; here and there she saw maps and pictures hung upon pegs. She took down a jar from one of the shelves as she passed; it was labelled 'Orange Marmalade', but to her great disappointment it was empty: she did not like to drop the jar for fear of killing somebody underneath, so managed to put it into one of the cupboards as she fell past it.

*From **Alice in Wonderland** by Lewis Carroll*

Architecture

The battle of the styles

Victorian buildings were often very grand. Architects liked two main styles for their designs:

> **Classical** – *using ideas from Ancient Greek buildings such as temples.*
> **Gothic** – *using ideas from buildings of the Middle Ages such as castles and cathedrals.*
> *The architects argued over which style was the best, and this became known as the 'battle of the styles'. Buildings in both styles can be found all over the country.*

❖ Look at these buildings. Which style do you think each one represents? Write your answer next to each one.

❖ Can you find any Victorian buildings in your area? Sketch or photograph them and make a display of classical or Gothic buildings.

Back in fashion

Many designs and styles that the Victorians liked are also popular today.

♣ The objects on this page can be found in sales catalogues. Do you have any objects like these in your home?

♣ Look through a catalogue that is no longer needed and cut out any objects that you think are Victorian in style.

♣ Why do you think these things are still popular today? What styles from the Victorian period do we not want to copy?

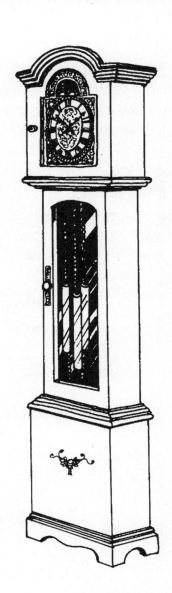

Language

Victorian street slang

The way people speak changes all the time and new words quickly come in and out of fashion. Below are listed some expressions used during Victorian times.

✤ How many of these words or phrases are still used today?

you got your fingers nipped – you have been in trouble

a dome-stick – a servant (from the word domestic)

cop – a policeman

shooter – a gun

silly coot – a stupid person

hansom cab – a horse-pulled taxi

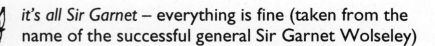

it's all Sir Garnet – everything is fine (taken from the name of the successful general Sir Garnet Wolseley)

a sip – a kiss

✤ Can you think of any words or phrases older people use that you wouldn't use?

✤ Write a crime story set on a Victorian street in 1890. Use as many of these words or phrases as you can. Begin: *The hansom cab stopped. A man with an eye-limpet got out...*

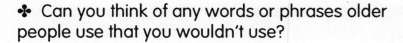

sick as a horse – very ill without being sick (horses can't vomit)

a rib bender – a blow on the ribs

a champion frost – a complete failure

cadger – a beggar

an eye-limpet – an artificial eye

rattled – very drunk

niner – a prisoner serving a nine year sentence

rave – like a lot

Make a music hall: 1

In Victorian times people went to the music hall to listen to music and other forms of entertainment.

✤ Make a model music hall as shown in the diagram on this page.

✤ Use plywood or stiff card for the walls to make them strong. Draw a background scene on paper, colour it in and stick it to the walls. (Remember to make your drawing the right size to fit the walls.)

✤ Now look at Make a music hall: 2. This sheet shows the characters and props for your music hall stage.

✤ Colour them in, then cut them out and stick them to card.

✤ Fix the figures to a piece of dowel or a long thin piece of card, so that you can move them around the stage easily. You can make extra characters if you wish.

✤ Design a poster for the music hall show. Make up names for the performers, such as 'The Amazing Addison Acrobats'.

✤ Perform your music hall acts for the rest of the class.

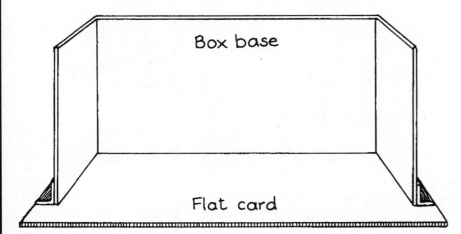

Entertainment

Make a music hall: 2

tree   gentleman   lady   child   strongman   clown   villain

flowers

picture frame

card

wooden block